pregnancy to school age

The Local BABY Directory™

Herts & Middlesex

4th edition

An A-Z of EVERYTHING
for
pregnant women, babies and children

edited by
Brigid Phillips

First published as the Harrow & Watford Baby Directory 1999
Second edition updated 2000
Third edition updated 2001
Fourth edition updated 2002

The Local Baby Directory
2 Field End Road, Pinner, Middlesex HA5 2QL. 020 8429 1849

ISBN 1-903288-08-8

Designed by LB Graphics, 01795 428150
Printed and bound in Great Britain by AOK Printers & Stationers, 01689 891460

The Local Baby Directory Herts & Middlesex edition
covers:
all of Hertfordshire and the postal county of Middlesex including the
towns and surrounding areas of Enfield, Edgware, Harrow, Hayes,
Pinner, Ruislip, Northwood, Uxbridge and Wembley.

Greater coverage of Southern Middlesex i.e. Hounslow, Twickenham and Staines
can be found in the Surrey edition of The Local Baby Directory.

Other Local Baby Directories now available:
Bristol, Bath & Somerset
Oxfordshire, Berks & Bucks
South Wales
Sussex & Hampshire
Surrey & S. Middlesex
and
The London Baby Directory

Franchise possibilities
If there is no Baby Directory in your area and you think
there should be,
contact us to discuss franchise opportunities.

Visit our website for
■ The Baby Directory Encyclopaedia of Pregnancy & Birth ■
■ Medical Advice ■ Breastfeeding ■
■ Educational Advice ■
■ Nanny Agency ■
■ Book Shop ■ Prizes ■ Updates ■

Brigid Phillips used to work in sales and marketing for a large multinational company before she gave it all up to be a 'full time mummy'. She has edited and produced 'Special Delivery', the newsletter of the Harrow branch of the National Childbirth Trust, and is currently their publicity officer. She now has two children, and a very messy house.

Acknowledgements
The Local Baby Directory, Herts & Middlesex would like to thank the following people for their help and support in its production: **Sarah Coyle** for a wonderful job of advertising sales and distribution, **Karen liebreich** for her inspiration and encouragement, **Sioux Peto** for her design skills, **Sue Budden** for her help in distribution, **Angela** and **Gail** for their co-franchisee encouragement, **Joanna, Aimee, Catriona** and **Elena** for their pictures, **Harrow NCT** for their continued support, all my **friends** for recommendations, advice and cups of coffee, **Mark** for all his support and **Joanna** and **Sam** without whom I would still be in a 'proper' job.

Welcome to the fourth edition of the Local Baby Directory: Herts & Middlesex - an A-Z information source of everything to do with pregnancy and your child's first few years in this area.

Our aim is to provide you with one convenient source of local information for all your needs while pregnant or as a parent or carer with a baby, toddler or child.

We have made no quality judgements about the entrants. The advertisers have paid to be included. Any omissions from the directory are either oversights on our behalf, or where we were unable to verify information. The accuracy of all the listings has been checked to the best of our ability, and we apologise for any mistakes that may have occurred.

Check out our web site at **www.babydirectory.com** which includes our **Encyclopaedia of Pregnancy and Birth**, as well as updated listings for the whole country, free medical advice, an excellent book shop and a nanny-finding facility.

I hope you find this Local Baby Directory very useful. Please let me know of any comments or improvements you would like to see in the next edition.

Brigid Phillips
Editor

Contact us for further details:
020 8429 1849
E-mail: localbabydirectory@blueyonder.co.uk
or see feedback page

To order, call our Credit Card hotline on **020 8429 1849**
or order via our secure website at **www.babydirectory.com**
or send this order form with your payment to:
The Local Baby Directory: Herts & Middlesex, 2 Field End Road, Pinner, Middlesex HA5 2QL

Title	Price	Qty	Postage	Total
The Local Baby Directory				
Herts & Middlesex (1-903288-08-8)	**£5.99**		**£1.00**	
Bristol, Bath & Somerset (1-903288-07-X)	£5.99		£1.00	
Surrey & S. Middlesex (1-903288-09-6)	£5.99		£1.00	
Oxfordshire, Berks & Bucks (1-903288-02-9)	£4.99		£1.00	
South Wales (1-903288-06-1)	£4.99		£1.00	
Sussex & Hampshire (1-903288-05-3)	£4.99		£1.00	
The London Baby Directory (1-90328810-X)	£8.99		£1.50	
	Total Order Value			

Please print clearly

Name . . . .

Address . . . .

. . . .

. . . . Postcode . . . .

Tel . . . . E-mail address . . . .

METHOD OF PAYMENT (*please tick appropriate box*)

Cheque/Postal Order ☐ Credit Card ☐

Please make cheques payable to **The Local Baby Directory**

Card Number ☐☐☐☐ ☐☐☐☐ ☐☐☐☐ ☐☐☐☐ ☐☐☐☐

Issue No ☐☐ Expiry Date ☐☐☐☐ Valid from ☐☐☐☐

Signature . . . .

Code . . . .   If you do not wish to receive further information please tick ☐

ADVERTISERS

If you provide a service or product we should know about, drop us a line, fax or e-mail. Listings are free, but we offer great advertising deals!

☐ This is a new product, service or facility.

☐ Please contact me with more information about advertising.

☐ Oops! You've missed this.

☐ Change of address, new branch, etc.

Category of product (eg, park, restaurant, nursery) ....

Name of product, service or facility ....

Address ....

....

Postcode .... Tel No ....

E-mail address .... www ....

Contact name and tel no *(if different from above)*

....

READERS

We would very much appreciate your comments. Errors, omissions, or poor service, please let us know. **A free copy of next year's book for the most useful comments!**

Feedback ....

....

....

....

Your own name, address, 'phone number, e-mail address (all optional)

....

....

Many thanks for taking the time to fill in this form
Please send completed form(s) to:
The Local Baby Directory: Herts & Middlesex
2 Field End Road, Pinner, Middlesex HA5 2QL
Tel: 020 8429 1849 E-mail: localbabydirectory@blueyonder.co.uk

acupuncture

(see also complementary health)

Some recommend acupuncture in pregnancy for morning sickness and turning breech babies

British Acupuncture Council
63 Jeddo Road, London, W12. 020 8735 0400
Ring for list of practitioners

adoption

Adoption UK
Manor Farm, Appletree Road, Chipping Warden, Banbury, Oxfordshire. 01295 660121

British Agencies for Adoption and Fostering
Skyline House, 200 Union Street, London, SE1
020 7593 2060

adventure playgrounds

(see also indoor adventure playcentres, parks & playgrounds)

These are usually for 5yrs and above. For the junior version, see indoor playcentres

Hemel Hempstead
Adeyfield Adventure Playground
Turners Hill
01442 242852

Bennetts End Adventure Playground
Rant Meadow
01442 242301

Chaulden (Shrub Hill) Adventure Playground
Long Chaulden
01442 213864

Grovehill/Woodhall Farm Adventure Playground
Star Cupid Green, rear of Redborne Road
01442 215872

Watford
Harebreak Adventure Playground
Leggatts Way, next to Bill Everett Centre
01923 677557
Toddler sessions Tues/Thurs/Fri

Harwoods Adventure Playground
Vicarage Road
01923 249001
Toddler sessions Mon/Tue/Thurs

after school clubs

Many schools run after school clubs for their own and external pupils, usually from 3.30-6pm. Try your child's school, your local school, or ring the local Youth Service *(see councils)*

Kids' Club Network Helpline
020 7512 2100
www.kidsclubs.org.uk

alexander technique

(see also exercise classes, personal trainers)

Society of Teachers of the Alexander Technique
129 Camden Mews, London, NW1
020 7284 3338

Visit us at

www.babydirectory.com

antenatal support & information

Information is available from your GP, your health clinic, the local maternity unit *(see hospitals)* and the organisations listed below

Active Birth Centre
25 Bickerton Road, London, N19
020 7482 5554

Independent Midwives' Association
01483 821104

National Childbirth Trust
Alexandra House, Oldham Terrace, London, W3. Enquiry Line: 0870 444 8707

antenatal teachers

(see also antenatal support & information)

Antenatal teachers are often affiliated to the National Childbirth Trust or the Active Birth Centre. Maternity hospitals usually offer classes. Book early

Enfield
Lola Alcaraz-Perez
020 8804 0328

Melbourn & Cambridge
Sharon Honig
01763 262906

St Albans
Julie Thomas
07779 032166

Stephie Shepherd
01727 753491
See advert on page 57

Watford
Karen Patrick
020 8882 5996

New Beginnings
01923 711908
Classes for first time couples run by midwives

antenatal testing

Ask your GP or maternity unit for information. Most tests are available on the NHS

Hitchin
Pinehill Hospital (BUPA)
01462 427203
Fetal viability, nuchal translucency, anomaly scan, amnio, CVS

London
Fetal Medical Centre
Devonshire Place
020 7486 0476

aquanatal

(see also leisure centres, swimming pools)

Hendon
Barnet Copthall Centre
020 8457 9900

Rickmansworth
William Penn Centre
01923 771050

St Albans
Aquanatal Classes
Townsend School
01727 811084

aromatherapy

(see also complementary health, massage)

AROMAKIDS
01278 671461
hippychick.ltd@virgin.net
www.hippychickproducts.com
Diverse range of essential-oil based toiletries for babies and toddlers

earth friendly baby
Healthquest Ltd, 7 Brampton Road, London, NW9. 020 8206 2066

Visit us at
www.babydirectory.com

International Federation of Aromatherapists
182 Chiswick High Road, London, W4
020 8742 2605

Pinner
Jo Raeburn
020 8429 8239

art

(see also arts centres, dance, drama, music)

Herts

ART ANGELS
Hitchin
01462 420862
Arts & craft workshops termtime/holidays,
Pre-school & school children

Colours you Choose
01923 440658
Paint your own pottery at home

Berkhamsted
The Making Place
196 High Street
01442 865661

Buntingford
Little People Art Group
01763 272269
1-5yrs

Cheshunt & Cuffley
Mucky Monkeys
01992 625405
18mths+. First session free.

Hitchin
Tim's Smart Art for Children
85 Tilehouse Street
01462 455376
7yrs+

Hoddesdon
Arts & Crafts
01992 447723
Paint your own pottery

Letchworth
The Place (Letchworth Arts Centre)
18-20 Leys Avenue
01462 670788
Sat am, 5-11yrs

St Albans
Children's Art
Maltings Arts Theatre
01727 844222
5yrs +

Crafty Capers Kids Club
Lemsford Road Scout Hut
01727 846590

Rainbow Tots
Trinity United Reform Church
01727 842573
2-4yrs

Stevenage
Kiddy Craft
01438 228337
2-5yrs

Tring
Creative Toddlers
Baptist Church, High Street
01494 758333

Watford
Hobbycraft
5 Century Park
01923 659000

Planet Ceramic
68 Market Street
01923 219182
Paint your own pottery

Middx

Edgware
Messy Play
020 8959 9045
18mths+

Paint Me Pottery
134 High Street
020 8931 0387
Paint your own pottery

art (cont.)

Greenford
Hobbycraft
Westway Cross Shopping Park
020 8747 7500

Harrow
Arty Toddlers
020 8909 9138
18mths-4yrs

Harrow Arts Centre
020 8428 0123
5-8yrs

Pinner
Adventures in Art
020 8621 3051
Holiday classes 5-12yrs

Messy Monkeys
020 8868 6674 / 8868 4862
18mths-4yrs

Ruislip
Paint the Plate
24 Victoria Road
01895 678221
Paint your own pottery

Temple Fortune
The Clay Café
8-10 Monkville Parade
020 8905 5353
Paint your own pottery

arts centres

Most produce children's shows in the holidays. May also run art, dance, drama, music classes. See these categories (*see also theatres*)

Barnet
The Bull Arts Centre
68 High Street
020 8449 0048

Harrow Weald
Harrow Arts Centre
356 High Road
020 8428 0123

Hemel Hempstead
Boxmoor Arts Centre
St Johns Road, Boxmoor
01442 233456

Hertford
Courtyard Arts Centre
Port Vale
01992 509596

Letchworth
The Place (Letchworth Arts Centre)
18-20 Leys Avenue
01462 670788

Radlett
Radlett Centre
1 Aldenham Avenue
01923 859291

www. BABY directory.com
Visit on-line for more ideas

astrological charts

Astrological Baby Profiles
32 High Street, Scotter, Lincs. 01724 761404

ChildStar
01473 240276

au pair agencies

(see also babysitters, childminders, nanny agencies)

Au pairs live-in and help with housework, childcare and babysitting. They are not generally recommended for very small babies

AA AU PAIRS (UK) LTD
01923 450714
AAAUPAIRS@aol.com
Professional Agency providing au-pairs to families in Herts, Middlesex and London

HANDIHELPS LTD
020 8386 8333
joy@handihelps.freeserve.co.uk
Supplying Au Pairs, Babysitters, Domestic Cleaners, Party helpers etc for 15 years

Angels International Au Pair Agency
020 8958 7002

Au Pairs & Nannies Direct
020 8905 4400

Au Pairs Plus
020 8905 4151

Golden Girls Au Pair Agency
020 8905 4152

Hammond Au Pair Agency
01442 863378

Ianda Au Pair Agency
020 8954 9900

Sunflower Au Pair Agency
01992 787389

Swedish Connection Au Pair Agency
020 8440 5288

baby research

BABYLAB
Centre for Brain & Cognitive
Development, FREEPOST,
32 Torrington Square,
London, WC1E 7JL
020 7631 6258
Have fun with your baby making discoveries about the brain

baby toiletries

Aromababy
2B Staley Street, Brunswick, Victoria,
Australia, 3056. 00 61 3 9387 1999
www.babyworkshop.com

earth friendly baby
Healthquest Ltd, 7 Brampton Road,
London, NW9 9BX. 020 8206 2066

babysitters

(see also childminders, nanny agencies)

SITTERS
0800 38 900 38
www.sitters.co.uk
SITTERS - the UK's leading and ONLY
national evening babysitting service

Childminders
6 Nottingham Street, London, W1
020 7935 3000

Handihelps Ltd
020 8386 8333
See advert on page 5

Lauren's Babysitting Services
Hertfordshire
07905 466640

bed wetting

Bed Wetting Clinic
Clementine Churchill Hospital, Sudbury Hill
020 8872 3843

benefits

Benefits Agency
Department of Social Security, CBC
Washington, Newcastle-upon-Tyne,
NE88 1AA. 08701 555501

Maternity Alliance
45 Beech Street, Barbican, London, EC2
020 7588 8582
Advice on benefits, maternity rights at work

birth announcements

(see also cards)

HAPPY HANDS
7 Brockwell Park Row, Tulse Hill,
London SW2
020 8671 2020
info@happyhands.ws
www.happyhands.ws

Chatterbox Cards
020 8650 8650
www.chatterboxcards.com
Personalised birth announcements and
christening invitations. Delivered in 3 days.
Free brochure

Please say you saw the ad in
The Local Baby Directory

CREATIVE CARDZ
8933 6080
www.creativecardz.com
See advert on page 11

Hyper Bubba
www.hyperbubba.com
Birth announcement websites

birth charts

Childstar
01473 240276

body painter

Body Artist for Pregnant Women
07803 121923
www.embody.org.uk
Become a canvas for the day and remember
your pregnancy forever

book clubs for children

Children First
Unit 6, The Carey Development, Tweed Road,
Clevedon
01737 833944

Letterbox Library
71-73 Allan Road, London, N16. 020 7503 4801

Red House Books Ltd
The Red House, Windrush Park, Witney,
Oxford. 01993 893472

books

Usborne Books at Home
020 8954 9376

book shops for children

Visit our website at
www.babydirectory.com for a selection of
the best children's books.

Herts

Barnet
Hammicks Bookshop
Unit 21, The Spires, High Street
020 8449 8229

W H Smith
1 The Spires Shopping Centre
020 8449 2144

Berkhamsted
The Bookstack
248 High Street
01442 864559

W H Smith
178-180 High Street
01442 871444

Bishops Stortford
Boardmans
14-16 North Street
01279 654033

Ottakar's
12 South Street
01279 508900

Cheshunt
Cheshunt Books
241 Turners Hill
01992 632501

Chorleywood
Chorleywood Bookshop
4 New Parade
01923 283566

Harpenden
The Bookstack
11 Bowers Parade
01582 715199

W H Smith
29 High Street
01582 460484

book shops for children (cont.)

Hatfield
Waterstone's
Units 7-8 The Galleria, Comet Way
01707 270161

Hemel Hempstead
Hammicks
Units 20-21, The Marlowes
01442 258200

W H Smith
181/183 The Marlowes
01442 263736

Hertford
Methven's Booksellers
12-14 Bircherley Green
01992 535136

W H Smith
24 Bircherley Green
01992 583230

Hitchin
Burgess Books
1a Churchyard 01462 452108

W H Smith
Unit 2, 121-123 Bancroft
01462 421133

Hoddesdon
The Book Centre
26 Falcon Walk
01992 467497

Letchworth
David's Bookshops
Childrens Books, 7 Eastcheap
01462 686764

W H Smith
21 Leys Avenue
01462 684415

Radlett
W H Smith
337 Watling Street
01923 856896

Rickmansworth
W H Smith
74 High Street
01923 772087

St Albans
Hammicks
8 St Peter's Street
01727 834966

Methven's Booksellers
17 The Maltings
01727 838011

Paton Books
34 Holywell Hill
01727 853984

W H Smith
25 Market Place
01727 853483

Waterstone's
8/10 Catherine Street
01727 868866

Stevenage
Ottakar's
1 The Forum
01438 355266

W H Smith
95 Queensway
01438 312137

Tring
Corbetts Bookshop (The Book Shop)
81 High Street
01442 826286

Waltham Cross
W H Smith
71 Waltham Cross Shopping Pavilion,
High Street
01992 761212

Ware
Ware Bookshop
10 Baldock Street
01920 463450

Watford
Books Books Books
136a High Street
01923 244274
Discount books

Visit us at
www.babydirectory.com

Bookworld
132 The Harlequin.
01923 213962
Discount books

Borders
201 High Street, Waterfields Retail Park
HQ: 020 7379 7313

W H Smith
54 The Harlequin
01923 211388

W H Smith
39 High Street
01923 225688

Waterstone's
174-176 The Harlequin
01923 218197

Welwyn Garden City
Maher the Bookseller
54 The Howard Centre
01707 373898

W H Smith
30 Howard Centre
01707 373686

Middlesex

Eastcote
Hammond Roberts
136 Field End Road
020 8868 5786

Edgware
Maher the Bookseller
Broadwalk Shopping Centre, Station Road
020 8951 5181

W H Smith
30 Broadwalk Shopping Centre, Station Road
020 8905 6188

Enfield
Ottakar's
26 Church Street
020 8363 6060

W H Smith
7-11 Palace Gardens Shopping Centre
020 8366 3633

Wesley Owen Books & Music
11 Cecil Road
020 8363 8517
Christian books

Harrow
Hammicks
60-62 St Ann's Road
020 8863 4578

W H Smith
14 St Anns Shopping Centre, St Anns Road
020 8863 9374

Hayes
Hayes Bookshop
6 Glebe Avenue
01895 637725

W H Smith
6 Station Road
020 8848 9884

Northwood
Northwood Bookshop
46 Green Lane
01923 826999

Pinner
Corbetts Bookshop
19-21 High Street
020 8866 1336

The Children's Bookshop
1 Red Lion Parade, Bridge Street
020 8866 9116

Ruislip
Corbetts Bookshop (The Bookshop)
51 High Street
01895 678269

The Bookstall
107 Victoria Road
01895 625727
Discount books

W H Smith
76 High Street
01895 632108

book shops for children (cont.)

Uxbridge
Bargain Books
3 Market Square
01895 257646

Barnard Bookshop
50 Windsor Street
01895 232751

Books etc
Unit 240a, The Chimes
01895 272800

James Thin
2a Mercer Walk, The Pavilions
01895 255969

Octagon Books
Pavilions Centre
01895 812626
Discount books

W H Smith
148 High Street
01895 256221

breastfeeding

Visit our website at
www.babydirectory.com for e-mail advice
and information from National Childbirth
Trust and Breastfeeding Network counsellors

Breastfeeding Network
0870 900 8787

Association of Breastfeeding Mothers
PO Box 207, Bridgewater, Somerset, TA6 7YT
020 7813 1481
24hr volunteer counselling service

La Leche League
BM Box 3424, London, WC1N 3XX
020 7242 1278
24hr counselling service

National Childbirth Trust Breastfeeding
Counsellors
0870 444 8708

cakes

Most cake shops also hire shaped tins for
birthday cakes

Bushey
Cakes of Good Taste
51 High Road
020 8950 0077

Cheshunt
Cake Base
21 High Street
01992 637900

Edgware
Clever Cakes
20 Churchill Road
020 8951 3402

Harrow
Freda's Cakes
24 Springfield Road
020 8424 2203

Hertford
The Sugarsmith
Post Office Walk, Fore Street
01992 500974

Northolt
Cake Makers Boutique
3 Station Parade, Ealing Road
020 8845 1037

Radlett
Louise's Simply Cakes
94 Watling Street
01923 859849

Ruislip
Icing on the Cake
81 Park Way
01895 622064

St Albans
The Cake Stand
The Maltings
01727 812913

Stevenage
Cakes of Joy
2 Baker Street, Middle Row
01438 726094

car seats & accessories

(see also nursery goods)

Baby's First Wave
www.babysfirstwave.com
The first drive home car flag

The In Car Safety Centre
5 Erica Road, Milton Keynes
01908 220909

Motorhoods (Colchester) Ltd
0800 163 725
Turns estate car into a 7 seater

Quickfit Safety Belt Centre
Inertia House, Lowther Road, Stanmore
020 8206 0101

Road Safety Enfield Council
Civic Centre, PO Box 52
020 8379 3638
Free service offering advice on children's car
sears, "try before you buy", checking existing
seats

cards

(see also birth announcements)

CREATIVE CARDZ
787 Kenton Lane, Harrow
020 8933 6080
www.creativecardz.com

CHATTERBOX CARDS
PO Box 142, Beckenham,
Kent, BR3 6ZL. 020 8650 8650
www.chatterboxcards.com
Personalised birth announcements and
christening invitations. Delivered in 3 days.
Free brochure

carriers

CHILD HIP SEAT
Hippychick Ltd, Barford Gables,
Spaxton, Bridgwater, Somerset
01278 671461
www.hippychickproducts.com
Innovative back-supporting belt with integral
seat for carrying children (6mths-3yrs).
Endorsed by osteopaths

Babyhut Ltd
PO Box 3401, Brighton BN1 3WE. 01273 245864
www.babyhut.net
Comprehensive range of 100% cotton baby slings,
baby hammocks & other natural products

Better Baby Sling
01923 444442
www.betterbabysling.co.uk
"Wonderfully easy to put on – very
comfortable" The Independent

Wilkinet
PO Box 20, Cardigan, SA43 1JB. 0800 138 3400

cassettes & CDs

Move & Groove with Paint Pots
020 7376 4571
32 songs for all ages

Cover to Cover Cassettes
PO Box 112, Marlborough,
Wiltshire, SN8 3UG. 01672 562255

castings

Casts, usually of hands or feet, preserved in
bronze, glass or on ceramic tiles

GOLDEN HANDS, SILVER FEET LTD.
Unit G. Homesdale Centre,
216-218 Homesdale Road, Bromley, Kent
www.goldenhands.co.uk

Happy Hands
7 Brockwell Park Row, Tulse Hill, London
020 8671 2020
www.happyhands.ws
Hand and foot prints and works of art
preserved on ceramic tiles

chemists, late opening

In case of emergency, police stations should
have information on local chemists which may
stay open late.

childcare listing magazine

Simply Childcare
16 Bushey Hill Road, London, SE5
020 7701 6111
www.simplychildcare.com

childminders

*(see also au pair agencies, babysitters, nanny
agencies)*

For lists of registered childminders in your
area, contact your local social services
department *(see councils)*

Childcare Link
www.childcarelink.gov.uk

www.childminders.co.uk
020 7487 4578

chiropractic

Suitable for treating back and neck pain. May
be useful for colic in babies

British Chiropractic Association
0118 950 5950

McTimoney Chiropractic Association
21 High Street, Eynsham, Oxfordshire
01865 880974

christening gowns

CHRISTENING GOWNS
35 Derwent Crescent, Kettering,
Northamptonshire. 01536 515401
julie@christeningoutfits.co.uk
www.christeningoutfits.co.uk
Over four hundred gowns and rompersuits in
stock, plus accessories

Thimbelina
7 Acremead Road, Wheatley, Oxfordshire
01865 872549
Hand-smocked heirloom gowns, outfits and
accessories handmade to order

cinemas

Many cinemas have a Saturday morning junior screening

circus workshops

Hemel Hempstead
Circus Unlimited
01442 213271
6yrs+

cleaners

(see also ironing services)

M & H HELPERS
020 8866 8276 or 020 8954 2647
MandHHelpers@tinyonline.co.uk
Reliable local cleaning and ironing service at reasonable rates

SELCLENE
01727 861001
For regular and reliable local cleaners and ironers.

SPIT 'N POLISH
01438 220384/07765 413412
For the best cleaners in town call us first …

clinics

Staffed by health visitors and community doctors, clinics provide health and development checks and are a good source of information and supplementary health care (e.g. family planning, chiropody, eye checks)

Please say you saw the ad in
The Local Baby Directory

clothing shops

(see also mail order: clothing, maternity wear, nearly new shops, nursery goods, shoe shops)

We have not listed the major chains, eg. Adams, Baby Gap, Hennes, John Lewis, Marks & Spencer, Monsoon, Mothercare, Next, etc which can be found in most high streets

Herts

Barnet
Village Wardrobe
259 East Barnet Road
020 8447 1338

Berkhamsted
Zebra
20a Lower Kings Road
01442 879997

Bishops Stortford
Lime Squash
8/9 Florence Walk, North Street
01279 501191

Borehamwood
Kindercare
116 Shenley Road
020 8953 2002

Bushey Heath
Little Poppits
23 High Road
8950 5058

Chorleywood
Hopscotch
7 Main Parade
01923 285235

Harpenden
Cherubs
78 High Street
01582 712309

Hatfield
Kid Kraft
92 The Galleria
01707 273020

Smarty
34 Town Centre
01707 263909

Hemel Hempstead
Ethel Austin Ltd
239 Edmonds Parade, Marlowes
01442 261292

Hansell & Grettel
23 Bennetts Gate
01442 252633

Hertford
Kids Connection
14 Market Place
01992 587466

Kings Langley
Nippers
19a High Street
01923 264099

Stevenage
Hey Baby
94 High Street
01438 216303

Jilly's
80-83 Market Square
01438 725259

Little Jems
26 The Glebe
01438 351104

Waltham Cross
Juniors
85 High Street
01992 788155

Togs
58 Bartholemew Court, High Street
01992 633279

Watford
Kids Styleast
41 Charter Place
01923 800843

Visit us at
www.babydirectory.com

Welwyn Garden City
Babyland
Unit 6, Garden Court, Tewin Road
01707 336714

Well In Kids
37 Fretherne Road
01707 392422

Middx

Edgware
Young Smartees
144 Burnt Oak Broadway
020 8952 7796

Bobbit & Doodles
1 Canons Corner
020 8905 4222

Enfield
Once upon a time
89 Lancaster Road
020 8363 5671

Harrow
C & S Discount Store
714-716 Kenton Road
020 8905 0585

Childrens Shop
264 Northolt Road, South Harrow
020 8422 3242

Hayes
Morsons Kids Clothing
Belmore Parade, 662 Uxbridge Road
020 8573 7548

Northwood Hills
Mini Modes Ltd
1-3 Joel Street
01923 826935

Pinner
Angels
363 Rayners Lane
020 8866 9972

Southall
C & S Discount Store
109 The Broadway
020 8574 3200

Cha-Cha
33 The Broadway
020 8574 2288

Uxbridge
Pumpkin Patch
225-226 The Chimes Shopping Centre
01895 252548

Wembley
Wonderland
548 High Road
020 8903 0617

clubs

(see also after school clubs)

Girl Guiding UK
020 7834 6242
www.guides.org.uk
Rainbows 5-7yrs, Brownies 8-12yrs

Scout Association
0845 300 1818
www.scoutbase.org.uk
Beavers 6-8yrs, Cubs 8-10yrs

Woodcraft Folk
London office: 020 8672 6031
www.poptel.org.uk/woodcraft

complementary health

(see also acupuncture, aromatherapy, craniosacral therapy, homeopathy, massage, osteopathy, reflexology, yoga)

Association of Systemic Kinesiology
020 8399 3215

Complementary Medicine Association (CMA)
020 8305 9571

Institute for Complementary Medicine
PO Box 194, London, SE16 1QZ
Send sae for list of local addresses

Little Miracles
PO Box 3896, London, NW3 7DS. 020 7431 6153
Flower essences - gentle remedies

complementary health (cont.)

National Institute of Medical Herbalists
01392 426022

Herts

Hertford
Hertford Natural Therapy
4 Old Cross
01992 589439

Hitchin
Hitchen Natural Therapy Centre
3-4 High Street
01462 459020

Letchworth
The Letchworth Centre
Rosehill Hospital, Hitchin Road
01462 678804

St Albans
Healing Hands
17 Russell Avenue
01727 833808

Middx

Eastcote
Field End Complementary Health Clinic
716a Field End Road
020 8422 4163

Edgware
Edgware Centre for Natural Health
128 High Street
020 8951 3475

Harrow
Waldron Studios, Holistic Education Centre
Waldron Road
020 8423 7635

Northwood
Alternatives Complementary Therapy Centre
118 High Street
01923 828832

computers for children

Edgware
Futurekids
170 Deans Lane
020 8906 8800

Pinner
Futurekids
10-12 Love Lane
020 8866 0100

Wembley
Futurekids
Wembley Point 1, Harrow Road
020 8900 5685

Herts

Watford
Ryde College
21-23 Greenhill Crescent,
Business Park
01923 255552
Toddler courses (18mths+)

concerts

West London Sinfonia
020 8997 3540
Big concert every Xmas

Barbican
020 7638 8891
LSO family concerts

cookery

Dodo Cookbook
PO Box 10507, London, N22 7WZ
0870 900 8004
www.dodopad.com

councils

Your local council is an excellent source of information. Ask for the Under 8s section, Early Years' section, or leisure. They can provide lists of local nurseries, childminders, schools, parks, etc.

Hertfordshire County Council
County Hall, Pegs Lane, Hertford
01992 555555
Children's Services or Childcare: Young in Herts
01438 737502 or 01923 471502
www.hertsdirect.org

London Borough of Barnet
The Town Hall, Hendon. 020 8359 2000
Children's Information Centre: The Old Town Hall, Friern Barnet Lane
0800 389 8312
www.barnet.gov.uk

London Borough of Brent
Town Hall, Forty Lane, Wembley
020 8937 1234
One Stop Shop (Information) 020 8937 1200
Children's Information Service: 020 8937 3001
www.brent.gov.uk

London Borough of Ealing
Perceval House, 14-16 Uxbridge Road, Ealing
020 8579 2424
Children's Information Service 020 8825 5588
www.ealing.gov.uk

London Borough of Enfield
Civic Centre, Silver Street, Enfield
020 8366 6565
Childcare Information Centre: 020 8482 1066
www.enfield.gov.uk

London Borough of Harrow
Civic Centre, Station Road, Harrow
020 8863 5611
Early Years & Childcare Service: 020 8861 5609
www.harrow.gov.uk

London Borough of Hounslow
Civic Centre, Lampton Road, Hounslow
020 8583 2000
Children's Information Service: 020 8583 3470
www.hounslow.gov.uk

London Borough of Hillingdon
Civic Centre, High Street, Uxbridge
01895 250111
Children's Information Service: 01895 277194
www.hillingdon.gov.uk

cradles

(see also nursery furniture & décor)

Swingers & Rockers
Terfyn Uchaf, Rhiw, Pwllheli, Gwynedd
01758 780305

craniosacral therapy

(see also osteopathy)

Craniosacral Therapy Association
07000 784735
www.craniosacral.co.uk

crèches, mobile

Mobile Crèche Company
020 8998 8255

cycling & cycling attachments

Christiania Tricycle
Zero Emissions 020 7723 2409
Family trailers

Visit us at
www.babydirectory.com

dance

(see also art, drama, gym, music)

Dance teachers often hold classes in different halls within a general area, so check neighbouring towns, as the teacher may be listed there. Most ballet classes are for children from 3years upwards unless otherwise stated

Herts

Abbots Langley
Rachelle School of Ballet
St Lawrence Church Hall
01923 243959

Ashwell
Ashwell School of Dance
07931 581665

Bishops Stortford
Bishops Stortford Dance Centre
Chritian Outreach Hall, Portland Road
01279 655522

Tracy Walker School of Dancing
Little Hallingbury
01279 501532

Borehamwood
Lila Vincent School of Dance & Drama
01923 857866

Broxbourne
Young Faries Ballet School
Grundy Park Leisure Centre
01992 634629

Buntingford
Premiere Schools of Dance and Drama
01992 578467

Tiffany's School of Dance
01763 281310
tap and modern

Bushey & Croxley Green
Rees Fisher School of Ballet
01494 792996

Bushey & Hemel Hempstead
Class Act Performing Arts
020 8891 6663

Bushey & Redbourn
MARGARET HOWARD THEATRE SCHOOLS
Harrison College, High Street
07000 863262
Performance in festivals, West End shows and lots of fun

Cheshunt
Ridgeway Studios
Fairley House, Andrews Lane
01992 633775

The Valle Academy
The Rosedale Centre, Andrews Lane
01992 622862

Chorleywood
Carol Kristian Theatre School
Memorial Hall
01923 284599

East Herts
Henningan O'Loughin Irish Dance Classes
01279 730053

Harpenden
Hiel'and Toe Club
Methodist Church Hall
01582 769607
Scottish dancing

Laura Cross School of Dancing
01582 763947

Louise Sheaves School of Dance
01582 766750

Hatfield
Splitz School of Dance and Drama
01438 814513

Hemel Hempstead
Betty Bouston Dance School
01442 212404

Carter School of Irish Dancing
01442 267269
Irish Dance from 4^1/$_2$yrs

Jayne Marie Dancing School
01442 217994

Judith Wallington School of Dancing
01442 267415

Potten End School of Ballet
01296 720875

Hemel Hempstead & Baldock
Starlight Dance Academy
01438 360811

Hertford
Carter School of Dancing
Sele Farm Community Centre, The Ridgeway
01992 581560

Letchworth
Dance Steps Academy
01462 642858

Michelle Gordine School of Dance
01462 487048
Disco, freestyle, streetdance

Potters Bar
FOOT-LIGHT SCHOOL
Wyllyotts Centre
020 8440 0881
www.thefootlightschool.co.uk

Potters Bar & Hoddesdon
Jean Wilson School of Dancing
07790 142657

Radlett
Radlett School of Dance
Watling Street
01582 733167

Rickmansworth
Collective Dance & Drama
The Studio, Rectory Lane
020 8428 0037

Royston
Barrett Smith School of Dance
01462 811149

Lisa Jane's School of Dance
01763 248220

Lisa Rusay Dance School
01763 260851
Russian style ballet

Stephanie Prior School of Dancing
The Studio, 21a Mill Road.
01763 246711
Freestyle disco, ballroom, latin, street

St Albans
Let's Dance
Marshalswick Baptist Church Hall,
The Quadrant
01727 875421

Pavely School of Dancing
Park Street Village Hall
01727 874278

Penny Waterman School of Dance
01727 858632

Stephanie Ledger School of Dancing
01582 715840

South Oxhey
Gypsy Booth School of Ballet & Theatre Arts
The Centre, Gosforth Lane
020 8428 3516

Stevenage & Aston
Footworks
01707 328441

Stevenage, Baldock, Hitchin, Stotfold
Andrew's Dance School
01767 601127

Visit us at

www.babydirectory.com

dance (cont.)

Stevenage, Welwyn Garden City, Wheathamstead
Joann Latus School of Dance
01582 620576

Tring
Shiny Shoes Dancing School
01296 580580

Ware
Chart Dancing
Wodson Park Sports Centre, Wadesmill Road
01920 487091

Welwyn & Kimpton
Dance Design
01727 839588

Welwyn Garden City
Top Hat Stage & Screen Schools
01707 394399

Welwyn, Digswell, Codicote
Caroline Shaw School of Dance
01438 746881

Middx

Barnet
Boden Studio
99 East Barnet Road
020 8449 0982

Parent & Toddler Dance
The Bull
020 8449 0048
18mths+

Highstone Dance Academy
020 8449 9305

Edgware
Chrystel Arts
15 Churchill Road
020 8952 1281

Eastcote & Pinner
MARGARET HOWARD THEATRE SCHOOLS
07000 863262
Performance in festivals, West End shows and lots of fun *See advert on page 18*

Harrow
Dance Classes
Harrow Arts Centre
020 8428 0123

The Eleonora Dance Studios
Harrow Weald
020 8427 1420

Lorna Clark School of Dancing
South Harrow Methodist Church,
Carlyon Lane, South Harrow
020 8866 2105

Ickenham
Suzanne's School
69 Swakeleys Road
01895 631858
Also tap & jazz

Northwood Hills
West London School of Dancing
St Edmunds Church Hall, Pinner Road
01923 820941

Pinner
Reddiford Studio School
38 Cecil Park
020 8866 0660

Queensbury
Beverley School of Dancing
Queensbury Methodist Church Hall,
Beverley Drive
01923 243976

Ruislip
The Maria Studio
120 Elliot Avenue, off Southbourne Gardens
01895 672301

Stanmore
The Van Niekerk Academy of Dance
020 8954 9921

Uxbridge
Hillingdon Theatre Dance Centre
01895 233988

Wembley
Minerva School of Ballet
St Cuthbert's Church Hall, Watford Road
020 8908 2167

dance-wear

Hitchin
Dance of Hitchin
102 Bancroft
01462 435988

Ickenham
Suzanne's Dance Supplies
69 Swakeleys Road
01895 631858

Welwyn Garden City
Top Hat Director's Studio & Dancewear Shop
17-19 Shoplands
01707 394399

designer outlets

Bicester Village
Bicester, Oxfordshire. 01869 323200

Great Western Designer Outlet
Kemble Drive, Swindon. 01793 507600
Junction 16, M4

designers

LB Graphics
01795 428150
sioux.lbgraphics@blueyonder.co.uk
Small business specialists

dolls' houses

Ruislip
OLD TRINKET BOX
1B High Street
01895 675658
Doll's houses and traditional toys
All your dolls house needs

Berkhamsted
Knit Knacks
2-4 Lower Kings Road
01442 870991

Hemel Hempstead
Enchanted Castles
64 High Street
01442 257678

Royston
Maple Street
Wendy
01223 207025

doulas

(see also midwives: independent)

A doula provides physical, emotional and practical support for the family during pregnancy, labour and immediately after

Doula UK
PO Box 33187, London, N8 9AW
www.doula.freeserve.co.uk

Matern'ali Yours
01480 407367
Doula Services

drama

Most take children from 5 years *(see also art, dance, gym, music and theatres which often run drama courses)*

Stagecoach
For details of your local teacher, ring national HQ on 01932 254333 or www.stagecoach.co.uk

Herts

Various venues
Top Hat Stage & Screen School
01707 394399

Barnet & Whetstone
Perform
020 7209 3805
4-7yrs

Susi Earnshaw Theatre School
020 8441 5010

Broxbourne
Jason Theatre School
01992 442439

Buntingford
Premiere Schools of Dance and Drama
01992 578467

Bushey
Margaret Howard Theatre Schools
07000 863262
See advert under dance

Bushey & Hemel Hempstead
Class Act Performing Arts
020 8891 6663

Bushey & Redbourn
Margaret Howard Theatre Schools
07000 863262
See advert under dance

Cheshunt & Cuffley
Ridgeway Studios
01992 633775

The Valle Academy
01992 622862

Chorleywood
Carol Kristian Theatre School
01923 284599

Hemel Hempstead
Boxmoor Drama
01442 233456

Hitchin
Market Theatre
Sun Street
01462 433553

Potters Bar
Capital Arts Theatre School
020 8449 2342

Rickmansworth
Blag Youth Theatre
01923 772320

Collective Dance & Drama
020 8428 0037

St Albans
Best Theatre Arts
01727 759634
www.besttheatrearts.com

Drama Classes
Maltings Arts Theatre
01727 844222

Drama Lessons
01727 867286

Theatrix Performing Arts
01727 760932

Visit us at
www.babydirectory.com

Sawbridgeworth
Youth CREATE
01279 721219
4-6yrs+

Sawbridgeworth & Much Hadham
Spotlight Theatre School
01799 541646
From 3yrs

Stevenage, Ware, Waltham Abbey
Jigsaw Arts
020 8447 4530
Weekend perfoming Arts schools

Ware
Premiere Schools of Dance and Drama
01992 578467

Welwyn Garden City
Lucia Knight Stage School
Barn Theatre
01707 331032

Middx

Enfield
Boden Studios
020 8367 2692

Jason Theatre School
01992 442439

Eastcote & Pinner
Margaret Howard Theatre Schools
07000 863262
See advert under dance

Edgware
Chrystel Arts
020 8952 1281

Harrow
Baby Bears
BearFoot Performing Arts School
01923 462960/644396

Harrow & Pinner
Perform
020 7209 3805
4-7yrs

Pinner
Naturama School of Drama
020 8866 5046

Ruislip
The Maria Studio
01895 672301

educational consultants

(see also helplines: education, schools, tuition)

Gabbitas Educational Consultants
Carrington House, 126-130 Regent Street,
London. 020 7734 0161
admin@gabbitas.co.uk
www.gabbitas.com
See under schools

ISCis London and South East
35-37 Grosvenor Gardens, London, SW1
020 7798 1560
Free handbook listing all accredited
independent schools

Society of Childhood Education
LBS Forum, 97 Cornwell Road, London SW7
020 020 7581 9357
www.societyofchildhoodeducation.com
A support and information society for
parents/guardians and nannies/au pairs;
members also include teachers, educational
experts

exercise for ante- and post-natal

(see also antenatal support & information, health clubs with crèches, leisure centres, swimming pools, yoga)

Local leisure centres and maternity hospitals
often hold exercise classes for new mothers

Guild of Postnatal Exercise Teachers
01453 884268
www.postnatalexercise.co.uk

KFA Classes
020 8692 9566
www.keepfit.org.uk
General exercise classes - phone for details of
your nearest class

exercise for ante- and post-natal (cont.)

Bishops Stortford
Lin'll Fix It
United Reformed Chuch Hall, Water Lane
01279 654902
P/N exercises. Crèche facilities

Enfield
Nina Quattrone
020 8367 6784

Hayes
Energize
Barnhill Community Centre, Ayles Road
020 8248 2738

Hitchin
Family Fitness
01462 621673
A/N & P/N. Crèche

Northwood & Pinner
Helen Stone
07973 890555
Dragons Health Club & Elliot Hall

Rickmansworth
Power Pushchair Walking
01923 441144

Pre and postnatal aerobics
01923 441144

St Albans
SK Aerobics
Brownie Hut, Waverley Road
01727 841281
Antenatal and postnatal (with chat)

ex-pat advice

American Women's Club of London
68 Old Brompton Road, London, SW7
020 7589 8292

Focus Information Services
13 Prince of Wales Terrace, London, W8
020 7937 0050

family planning

Your GP or local hospital (*see hospitals*) can advise on your nearest family planning clinic, or may provide the service themselves

fancy dress

mail order

Charlie Crow
01782 417133

Fairytales
PO Box 21220, London, W9 1ZE
020 7286 7142

Fancy Days
020 8675 9160
Make your own costumes

Hopscotch
61 Palace Road, London, SW2
020 8674 9853

retail

Berkhamsted
ABC Costume Hire
211 High Street
01442 863786

Eastcote
Sniggers Party Shop
103 Field End Road
020 8868 7323

Hertford
Party World
20 St Andrew Street
01992 553618

Hitchin
Dance of Hitchin
102 Bancroft
01462 435988

Stevenage
Festival Costumes
rear of 160 High Street, Codicote
01438 820967

Ware
Carnival Fancy Dress Hire
12-13 Becketts Walk
01920 461394

Watford
Masquerade
8 Langley Road
01923 243842

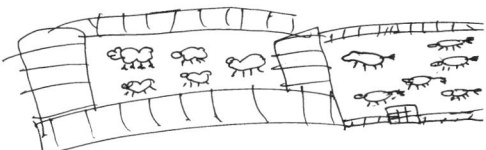

farms

(see also outings, zoos)

In addition to animals, most offer play areas
and cafes

Herts

Bushey
Animal World
21 Lincolnsfield
01923 219902
Can be combined with Activity World

Elstree
Aldenham Country Park
Dagger Lane
020 8953 9602
Entrance free but take three £1 coins for
parking

Hitchin
Waterhall Farm and Craft Centre
Whitwell
01438 871256

Kings Langley
Langleybury Childrens Farm
Langleybury Lane
01923 270603
Open weekends, Easter-Oct

Letchworth
Standalone Farm
Wilbury Road
01462 686775
Mar-Sept

London Colney
Willows Farm Village
Coursers Road
01727 822444

Royston
Wimpole Home Farm
Grounds of Wimpole Hall, on A1189
01223 207257
Mar-Nov

Waltham Abbey
Lee Valley Park Farm
Stubbings Hall Lane, Crooked Mile
01992 892781

Middx

Feltham
Hounslow Urban Farm
Faggs Road
020 8751 0850
Feb-Oct, Tues-Sun

Further afield
Bedfordshire

Nr. Leighton Buzzard
Mead Open Farm
Stanbridge Road, Billington
01525 852954

Visit us at
www.babydirectory.com

farms (cont.)

Thurleigh
Thurleigh Farm Centre
Cross End
01234 771597

Buckinghamshire

Aylesbury
Oak Farm Rare Breeds park
Broughton
01296 415709

High Wycombe
Odds Farm Park
Wooburn Common
01628 520188

Luton
Woodside Animal Park
Mancroft Road, Slip End Village
01582 841044

Stoke Mandeville
The Bucks Goat Centre
Layby Farm
01296 612983

Essex

Epping
Hobbs Cross Open Farm
Theydon Garnon
01992 814862

South Woodham Ferrers
Marsh Farm County Park
01245 321552

fatherhood

(see also helplines)

www.fathersdirect.com

Visit us at
www.babydirectory.com

financial advice

TUNBRIDGE WELLS EQUITABLE FRIENDLY SOCIETY
Abbey Court, St John's Road,
Tunbridge Wells, Kent
01892 515353
www.twefs.co.uk

Family Assurance Friendly Society
0800 616695

Friends Provident
United Kingdom House, 72-122 Castle Street,
Salisbury. 01722 318000

IFG Financial Services Ltd
Trinity House, Anderson Road, Swavesey,
Cambridgeshire. 01954 233555

Invesco Europe
11 Devonshire Square, London. 020 7626 3434

John Charcol Ltd
0800 718191

Jump
0800 082 8180

Royston Fox
Russell Fox Nori, 117 Piccadilly, Mayfair,
London W1. 020 7744 6556

first aid courses

Your local NCT may also run infant first aid
courses *(see antenatal support)*

The Parent Company
020 7935 9635

Safe & Sound
020 8449 8722

Harrow
British Red Cross
39 Sheepcote Road
020 8427 8788
Run general first aid courses and a 2 hour
infant resuscitation class

Hemel Hempstead, Hertford, Stevenage
St John Ambulance
01438 740044
Courses for babies and children

flower remedies

Little Miracles
PO Box 3896, London, NW3 7DS
020 7431 6153

food

(see also nutrition, organic, pubs, restaurants)

BABYNAT
0118 951 0518
www.organico.co.uk
Organic follow-on milk available from organic
& healthfood shops or direct mail

Truuuly Scrumptious Organic
01761 239300
www.bathorganicbabyfood.co.uk

Please say you saw the ad in
The Local Baby Directory

football

(see also leisure centres)

Abbots Langley
Fun Football
YMCA Woodlands
01923 662222

Bishops Stortford
The Football Shop
65 South Street
01279 501009

Cheshunt
Soccer Tots
Goffs Sport Centre
01992 629688

Hoddesdon
Soccer Tots
John Warner Sports Centre, Stansted Road
01992 445375

football (cont.)

Pinner
Total Football
438 Rayners Lane
020 8429 1661

South Ruislip
Queensmead Sports Centre
Victoria Road
020 8845 6010

Stanmore
Elms Soccer
020 8954 8787

Watford
Football in the Community
Watford Football Club, Vicarage Road
Stadium
01923 440449

Junior Football Course
Bill Everett Community Centre
01923 441444

footprints

(see also art)

FOOTPRINTS
Baby-feet at home
020 7736 2157
www.baby-feet.com
Create a lasting memento of your baby's
footprints on pottery - £29

french classes & clubs

LA JOLIE RONDE
01949 839715
info@lajolieronde.co.uk
www.lajolieronde.co.uk
French for children 3-11yrs. Classes
throughout the UK

Le Club Français
01962 714036
Phone for details of local classes

Harrow
Les Pitchouns
020 8863 2998
4-10yrs

Harrow & Stanmore
Jeux d'Enfants
020 8427 3678
5yrs+

Pinner
La Farandole
01923 841852
Group for bi-national children

Northwood
Les Petits Ecoliers
01923 841852
4-8yrs

Ware & Wormley
La Farandole
01920 871279

gifted children

Gifted Monthly Magazine
07887 923165
www.giftedmonthly.com

National Association for Gifted Children
0870 770 3217

gifts

(see also mail order)

local companies

ROSE ROCHE
Harrow
020 8933 3230
roches@supanet.com
Exclusive hand painted personalised keepsake
boxes and gifts for children

Ruislip
Old Trinket Box
1B High Street
01895 675658
Personalised baby memento boxes. Other
christening gifts
See advert on page 21

other areas

DODOPAD
PO Box 10507, London, N22 7WZ
0870 900 8004
www.dodopad.com
Indodispensible family organiser in desk,
calendar & pocket formats - practical & fun -
plus much more…

GOLDEN HANDS, SILVER FEET LTD.
Unit G. Homesdale Centre, 216-218
Homesdale Road, Bromley, Kent
020 8290 4091
www.goldenhands.co.uk
Your hands and feet captured in bronze, brass,
aluminium or stone …. Forever

I LOVE BALLOONS LTD
020 8904 0004
www.Iloveballoons.co.uk
Beautiful balloons bouquet deliveries for
newborn babies and birthdays

KITTY'S ANTIQUE PRINTS & MAPS
5 Monks Drive, London W3
020 8992 5104
www.kittyprint.com
The perfect personal gift for every occasion

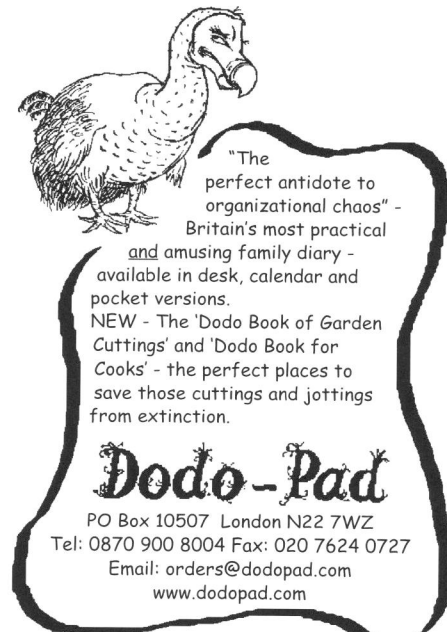

"The perfect antidote to organizational chaos" - Britain's most practical <u>and</u> amusing family diary - available in desk, calendar and pocket versions.
NEW - The 'Dodo Book of Garden Cuttings' and 'Dodo Book for Cooks' - the perfect places to save those cuttings and jottings from extinction.

Dodo-Pad
PO Box 10507 London N22 7WZ
Tel: 0870 900 8004 Fax: 020 7624 0727
Email: orders@dodopad.com
www.dodopad.com

Glittergifts
www.glittergifts.co.uk

Happy Hands
020 8671 2020
www.happyhands.ws

Little Angel
01473 323146
www.littleangel.info

Stork Express
PO Box 150, Amersham, Buckinghamshire,
HP7 0TH
01494 434294
www.storkexpress.co.uk

Personal Presents Ltd
Unit 4, Hartley Place, Church Lane, Wexham,
Berkshire. 0870 7271 884

Serena Harrison's Gifts for Godchildren
01249 821019

Please say you saw the ad in
The Local Baby Directory
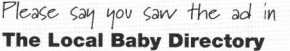

gym

Many local leisure centres also offer gym classes *(see also leisure centres)*

Tumbletots
National enquiries: **0121 585 7003**

Local class enquiries:
Bishops Stortford
01279 411875
Harrow
020 8958 6579
Hemel Hempstead
01296 394709
Palmers Green
020 8372 2147
Potters Bar
01992 447955
Stevenage
01438 369848
Uxbridge
01753 650671
Watford
01727 824259

Herts

Borehamwood
Fizzifun
The Venue, Potters Lane
020 8386 9886
Crawling to walking

Kidazz
020 8207 6903

Bushey
Fizzifun & Gymtots
Bushey Grove Leisure Centre, Aldenham Road
01923 470140

Tearless & Fearless
01923 221801

Harpenden
Harpenden Gym Club
Guide HQ, Townsend Lane. 01582 461488
2-5yrs

Hatfield
Flip Tots & Tiny Moves
Hatfield Leisure Centre, Travellers Lane
01707 268769

Potters Bar
Fizzifun
Furzefield Centre, Mutton Lane
01707 850500

Radlett
Tearless & Fearless
01923 221801

St Albans
Pre School Gym & Kinder Gym
Bricket Wood Sports Centre, Smug Oak Lane,
Bricket Wood
01923 662224
From walking. Kinder gym 3-5yrs

Sporty Tots
Sandringham School
01727 811084

Stansted Abbotts
Frisky Feet Music & Movement
01920 877606
18mths-4yrs, half gym, half music sessions

Ware
Action Tots
Woodson Park Sports Centre, Wadesmill Road
01920 467194

Watford
Kindergym
Watford Leisure Centre, Horseshoe Lane
01923 670644
Kindergym for walking to 2yrs

Welwyn Garden City
Jellie Beans & Tiger Tots
Gosling Sports Park
01707 384308

Visit us at
www.babydirectory.com

Middx

Various venues
Kidazz
020 8866 8171

Enfield
Little Steps Gym
St Stephens Church, Park Avenue,
Bush Hill Park
020 8482 1485

Hayes
Little Steps Gym
The Scouts Centre, The Barn, High Street,
Harlington
01753 674150
www.firststepsgym.bizland.com

Harrow
Harrow School of Gymnastics
next to Harrow Leisure Centre,
Christchurch Avenue
020 8427 5611
Play gym for under 5's, structured classes from
3yrs

West London YMCA
Victoria Halls, Sheepcote Road
020 8427 8041

Ruislip
Swallows Gym
The Dome (opposite Sainsburys),
South Ruislip
020 8841 6666
Parent & toddlers drop in sessions

hairdressers

Many hairdressers have a special chair
attachment, and offer a cheap cut for kids.
Then again there's always the pudding basin
and a pair of scissors

health clubs with crèches

Local authority sports centres also often
provide crèches to supplement their sports
activities. *(see leisure centres, swimming pools)*

Herts

Berkhamsted
Fitness First Health Club
172-176 High Street
01442 878000

Bishops Stortford
Cannons Health Club
Anchor Street
01279 507002

Bushey
David Lloyd Club
Hartspring Lane
01923 213760

Borehamwood
Holmes Place
84 Shenley Road
020 8207 0020

Hoddesdon
Good Health Club
39 Chaucer Way
01992 440255

Physical Limit
Clockhouse Building, Brewery Road
01992 444019
Supervised playroom

Potters Bar
Sportz Academy
Byng Drive
01707 660777

Rickmansworth
The Fitness Centre
Rickmansworth Sports Club, Park Road
01923 710676

St Albans
Batchwood Tennis & Golf Centre
Batchwood Drive
01727 844250

The friendly face of Health & Fitness

- **Air Conditioned Gym**
- **20 m swimming pool**
- **Free Studio classes**
- **6 Squash Courts**
- **2 Crèches** (3mth – 6 yrs)
- **Spa, Sauna & Steam room**
- **Beauty & Physio Rooms**
- **Bar & Bistro**

For further details Call:
01923 840214
Chestnut Avenue, Northwood
Middlesex, HA6 1HR

health clubs with crèches (cont.)

Cannons Health Club
Nightingale Lane
08707 582113

Stevenage
David Lloyd Leisure Club
Stevenage Leisure Park, Kings Way
01438 847000

Odyssey Knebworth
Old Knebworth Lane
01438 313320

The Factory
Units 1-2, Wedgewood Gate, Wedgewood Way
01438 749444

Tring
Exclusively Ladies
68-70 Mortimer Hill
01442 828881

Watford
Watford YMCA Fitness
Watford YMCA Charter House, Charter Place
01923 353607

Middx

Brentford
Top Notch Health Club
Windsor Close
020 8569 8225

Enfield
David Lloyd Health & Fitness
180 Carterhatch Lane
020 8364 5858

Greenford
Boots Wellbeing Centre
Westway Cross Retail Park
0845 121 9000

David Lloyd Ealing
Greenford Road
020 8422 7777

Hounslow
David Lloyd Health & Fitness Club
Southall Lane
020 8573 9378

Northolt
Dragons Health Club
Rowdell Road, Western Avenue
020 8841 5611

Northwood
DRAGONS HEALTH CLUB
Chestnut Avenue
01923 840214
Excellent crèche (from 3 months), gym, pool & exercise classes

Riverside Club
Ducks Hill Road
01923 848000

Uxbridge
Holmes Place
Vine Street
01895 270044

Virgin Active
Stockley Park
0845 130 1777

West Drayton
Spring Health Leisure
422 Bath Road
020 8897 6001

helplines

If you can't find what you're looking for here, try the index at the back of the book

aids
Positively Women. 020 7713 0222

Sexual Health & National Health Helpline
0800 567123
Information on aids and sexually transmitted diseases

allergy
British Allergy Foundation. 020 8303 8583
www.allergyfoundation.com

anaphylaxis
Anaphylaxis Campaign. 01252 542029
www.anaphylaxis.org.uk
Severe allergic reactions, e.g. nuts

asthma
National Asthma Campaign. 020 7226 2260
www.asthma.org.uk

autism
National Autistic Society. 020 7833 2299
www.nas.org.uk

bedwetting
Bedwetting Education Advisory Line
0800 085 8189

Enuresis Resource & Information Centre (ERIC). 0117 960 3060
www.eric.org.uk

bereavement
Child Bereavement Trust. 01494 446648
www.childbereavement.org.uk

Child Death Helpline. 0800 282 986

CRUSE Bereavement Care. 020 8940 4818

Stillbirth and Neonatal Death Society (SANDS). 020 7436 7940
www.uk-sands.org
Information and support for bereaved parents

birth
Birth Crisis Network. 01865 300266

Birth Defects Foundation. 08700 707020

National Childbirth Trust. 0870 4448707

blindness
LOOK (National Federation of Families with Visually Impaired Children. 0121 428 5038

RNIB. 020 7391 2245

brain damage
British Institute for Brain Injured Children
01278 684060
www.bibic.org.uk

bullying
Anti-Bullying Campaign. 020 7378 1446
For children bullied at school.

Kidscape. 020 7730 3300
www.kidscape.org.uk

caesarians
Caesarian Support Network. 01624 661269
6pm-10pm, weekends

cerebral palsy *See also main entry*
Cerebral Palsy Helpline (SCOPE)
0808 800 3333
www.scope.org.uk
Mon-Fri, 9am -9pm; w/e 2 -6pm

childcare
Daycare Trust. 020 7840 3350
National childcare campaign

Home-Start UK. 020 7388 6075
www.home-start.org

children
ChildLine. 0800 1111
www.childline.org.uk

cleft lip
Cleft Lip and Palate Association (CLAPA)
020 7431 0033
www.clapa.com

coeliac disease
Coeliac UK. 01494 437278

cot death
Cot Death Helpline. 0845 601 0234

Cot Death Society. 01925 850086
www.cotdeathsociety.co.uk

Visit us at
www.babydirectory.com

helplines (cont.)

Foundation for the Study of Infant Deaths
020 7233 2090
www.sids.org.uk/fsid

cruelty
NSPCC Child Protection Helpline
0800 800 500

crying babies
Serene (incorporating Cry-sis). 020 7404 5011
Helpline 8am-11pm

cystic fibrosis
Cystic Fibrosis Trust. 020 8464 7211
www.cftrust.org.uk

deafness
National Deaf Children's Society
020 7250 0123

diabetes
Diabetes UK
(ex-British Diabetes Association)
020 7323 1531
www.diabetes.org.uk

disability
Contact-A-Family. 020 7383 3555
www.cafamily.org.uk
Local parent support groups

Council for Disabled Children. 020 7843 6000
www.ncb.org.uk

Disability Alliance. 020 7247 8763
Advice on rights

Scope. 020 7619 7100
www.scope.org.uk/

divorce
Mediation in Divorce. 020 8891 6860

down's syndrome
Down's Heart Group. 01525 220379

Down's Syndrome Association. 020 8682 4001
www.dsa.uk.com

dyslexia
British Dyslexia Association. 0118 966 8271
See also reading difficulties

dyspraxia
Dyspraxia Foundation. 01462 454986
For help with 'Clumsy Child Syndrome'

eczema
National Eczema Society. 020 7388 4097
www.eczema.org

education
British Association for
Early Childhood Education. 020 7539 5400
www.early-education.org.uk

Children's Information Service. 0800 960296
www.childcarelink.gov.uk

Home Education Advisory Service
01707 371854
www.heas.co.uk

ISCis: London & South East. 020 7798 1560
www.iscis.uk.net/southeast

endometriosis
National Endometriosis Society
020 7222 2781
www.endo.org.uk

The SHE Trust
(Simply Holistic Endometriosis)
01522 519992
www.shetrust.org.uk

epilepsy
British Epilepsy Association. 0113 210 8800
www.epilepsy.org.uk

fatherhood
Families Need Fathers. 020 7613 5060
www.fnf.org.uk
Advice for non-custodial parents

formula milk
Baby Milk Action. 01223 464420
www.babymilkaction.org

fragile X
Fragile X Society. 01424 813147

health
Group B Strep Support. 01444 416176
www.gbss.org.uk

Visit us at
www.babydirectory.com

NHS Direct. 0845 4647
www.nhsdirect.nhs.uk
24-hr line

Women's Health. 020 7251 6580
www.womenshealthlondon.org.uk
Gynaecological and sexual health. Reference
library and advice

herpes
Herpes Viruses Association. 020 7609 9061

hyperactivity
Hyperactive Children's Support Group
01903 725182
10am-1pm

learning difficulties
British Institute for Learning Disabilities
01562 723010

marriage
National Family Mediation. 020 7383 5993

Relate: National Marriage Guidance
020 8367 7712
www.relate.org.uk

maternity
Assoc for Improvements in Maternity
Services AIMS. 020 8390 9534
www.aims.org.uk

ME
Action for ME Pregnancy Network
01749 670799
www.afme.org.uk

meningitis
Meningitis Research. 08088 003344
www.meningitis.org

Meningitis Trust. 0845 600 0800
www.meningitis-trust.org.uk

miscarriage
Miscarriage Association. 01924 200799
www.miscarriageassociation.org.uk

motherhood
Meet a Mum Association (MAMA)
01761 433598
www.mama.org

multiple births
Multiple Births Foundation. 020 8383 3519
www.multiplebirths.org.uk

parenthood
National NEWPIN. 020 7358 5900

Parentline Plus. 0808 800 2222
www.parentlineplus.org.uk
For parents under stress

postnatal depression
Association for Postnatal Illness
020 7386 0868
www.apni.org

pre-eclampsia
Action on Pre-Eclampsia (APEX helpline)
020 8427 4217
Calls 10am-1pm

reading difficulties
National Advice Centre for Children with
Reading Difficulties. 0845 604 0414

sexual abuse
SACCAA. 020 8950 7855

sick children
Action for Sick Children. 0800 074 4519

single parents
National Council for One-Parent Families
0800 185026
www.oneparentfamilies.org.uk

stammering
British Stammering Association
020 8983 1003
www.stammering.org

twins
Twins and Multiple Births. 01732 868 8000
Helpline only 7-11pm evenings and weekends.
Weekdays: 0151 348 0020

violence
Women's Domestic Violence Helpline
0161 839 8574
www.wdvh.org.uk

working parents
Parents at Work. 020 7628 2128
www.parentsatwork.org.uk

hiring equipment

(see also nearly new shops, party equipment)

LITTLE STARS
020 8621 4378 or 8537 0980
www.littlestars.co.uk
Buy or hire your new baby equipment today

holiday play schemes

(see also art, football, etc)

Local councils often run grant-aided holiday schemes. Independent schools, leisure centres, swimming pools and private companies offer their own programmes

Aspire Summer Camp
020 8420 6731
Fully integrated camp for able bodied / disabled

Barracudas
Bridge House, Bridge Street,
St Ives, PE27 5EH
01480 467567

Camp Beaumont
11 Prince of Wales Road, Norwich
0845 608 1234

EAC Activity Camps
0845 113 0022

PGL Travel Ltd
Alton Court, 10 Yard Lane, Ross-on-Wye,
Herefordshire
0500 749147
6yrs+

The Centre Holiday Playscheme
South Oxhey
020 8428 4954

home birth

(see also antenatal support & information advice)

National Childbirth Trust branches often have a home birth support group. If you get no joy from your GP, contact your local hospital's Director of Midwifery *(see hospitals)* or an independent midwife *(see midwives)*

homeopathy

(see also complementary health)

College of Practical Homeopathy
020 8445 6123
For a list of medically qualified homeopaths, doctors and dentists

Society of Homeopaths
4a Artizan Road, Northampton. 01604 621400

United Kingdom Homeopathic Medical Association
6 Livingstone Road, Gravesend, Kent
01474 560336

hospitals: dolls & teddies

The Doll and Teddy Hospital and Orphanage
Old Hill House, 53 Dover Street,
Maidstone, Kent. 01622 727020

The Doll's Hospital
17 George Street, Hastings. 01424 444117

hospitals: NHS

In case of emergency call 999

Barnet
Barnet Hospital
Well House Lane. 020 8216 4000

Edgware
The Birth Centre
Edgware Hospital, Burnt Oak Broadway
020 8732 6777 / 6669
birthcentre.co.uk
Midwife led unit

Enfield
Chase Farm Hospitals NHS Trust
The Ridgeway. 020 8366 6600

Harrow
Northwick Park & St Marks Hospital
Watford Road, Harrow. 020 8864 3232
Supervisor of Midwives: 020 8869 2885

Hemel Hempstead
Hemel Hempstead General Hospital
Hillfield Road. 01442 287034

Hillingdon
Hillingdon Hospital
Pield Heath Road. 01895 238282

Isleworth
West Middlesex Hospital
Twickenham Road. 020 8560 2121

Park Royal
Central Middlesex Hospital
Acton Lane. 020 8965 5733

St Albans
St Albans City Hospital
Waverlye Road. 01727 866122
Antenatal checks only - maternity unit at
Hemel Hempstead

Southall
Ealing Hospital
Uxbridge Road. 020 8574 2444

Stevenage
Lister Hospital
Coreys Mill Lane. 01438 314333

Watford
Watford General Hospital
Vicarage Road
01923 244366

Welwyn Garden City
Queen Elizabeth II Hospital
Howlands. 01707 328111

hospitals: private maternity

Many of the NHS hospitals also have private wards, which may ensure some extra privacy and comfort. See above for contact details

Hospital of St John & St Elizabeth
Grove End Road, London, W8
020 7286 5126

Portland Hospital
205-209 Great Portland Street, London, W1
020 7580 4400

hotels & holidays

(see also ski companies, travel companies specialising in children, travel with kids)

The following offer special facilities for children and babies, ranging from crèches to child listening, playgrounds, pools, etc

Centerparcs Ltd
0990 200200

Avon
The Bath Spa Hotel
Sydney Road, Bath. 01225 444424

Channel Islands
Stocks Island Hotel
Manor Valley, Sark. 01481 832001

Clwyd
Oriel House Hotel
Upper Denbigh Road, St. Asaph. 01745 582716

Co.Durham
Redworth Hall Hotel
Redworth, Nr Newton Aycliffe. 01388 772442

hotels & holidays (cont.)

Cornwall
FOWEY HOTEL
Hanson Drive, Fowey. 01726 833866
www.luxuryfamilyhotels.com
Play area, crèche, indoor pool

Bedruthan Steps Hotel
Mawgan Porth. 01637 860555

Carlyon Bay Hotel
Sea Road, St Austell. 01726 812304

Cawsand Bay Hotel
Cawsand, Torpoint. 01752 822425

Coombe Mill
St. Breward. 01208 850344

Long Cross Hotel
Trelights, Port Isaac. 01208 880243

Penmere Manor Hotel
Mongleath Road, Falmouth. 01326 211411

Polurrian
Mullion. 01326 240421

Sands Family Resort
Watergate Road, Porth. 01637 872864

Tredethy House Country Hotel
Helland Bridge, Bodmin. 01208 841262

Watergate Bay Hotel
Watergate Bay, Newquay. 01637 860543

Whipsiderry Hotel
Trevelgue Road, Porth, Newquay
01637 874777

Wringford Down Hotel
Cawsand. 01752 822287

Cumbria
Allerdale Court Hotel
Market Place, Cockermouth. 01900 823654

Armathwaite Hall Hotel
Nr. Keswick. 01768 776551

Castle Inn Hotel
Bassenthwaite, Keswick. 01768 776401

Hilton Keswick Lodore
Borrowdale Road, Keswick. 01768 777285

Devon
LANGSTONE CLIFF HOTEL
Mount Pleasant Road, Dawlish Warren,
Dawlish. 01626 868000
reception@langstone-hotel.co.uk
www.langstone-hotel.co.uk
19 acres of woodland, children's suppers,
indoor and outdoor pools, tennis, therapy
rooms, go karts

Boswell Farm
Sidford. 01395 514162

The Bulstone Hotel
Higher Bulstone, Branscombe, Sidmouth
01297 680446

Radfords County Hotel
Dawlish. 01626 863322

Thurlestone Hotel
Thurlestone. 01548 560382

Dorset
KNOLL HOUSE
Studland Bay. 01929 450450
enquiries@knollhouse.co.uk
www.knollhouse.co.uk
Gardens, pools, tennis, golf, health spa,
playroom, children's restaurant, adventure
playground

MOONFLEET MANOR
Moonfleet, Nr Weymouth. 01305 786948
www.luxuryfamilyhotels.com
Play area, crèche, extensive leisure facilities
including indoor pool

Chine Hotel
25 Boscombe Spa Road, Bournemouth
01202 396234

Fairfields Hotel
Studland Bay. 01929 450224

Hotel Buena Vista
Pound Street, Lyme Regis. 01297 442494

Sandbanks Hotel
15 Banks Road, Sandbanks, Poole
01202 707377

Dyfed
Hotel Penrallt
Aberporth, Cardigan. 01239 810227

Please say you saw the ad in
The Local Baby Directory

hotels & holidays (cont.)

East Lothian
Maitlandfield House Hotel
24 Sidegate, Haddington. 01620 826513

Essex
Churchgate Manor Hotel
Churchgate Street, Old Harlow. 01279 420246

Flintshire
St. David's Park Hotel
Ewloe. 01244 520800

Gloucestershire
Calcot Manor
Tetbury. 01666 890391

Gwynedd
Trefeddian Hotel
Aberdyfy. 01654 767213

Hampshire
Watersplash Hotel
The Rise, Brockenhurst. 01590 622344

Hertfordshire
Marriott Hanbury Manor
Nr Sandridge, Ware. 01920 487722

Inverness
Polmaily House Hotel
Drumnadrochit, Loch Ness. 01456 450343

Isle of Wight
The Clarendon Hotel - The Wight Mouse Inn
Chale. 01983 730431

Priory Bay Hotel
Eddington Road, St. Helens
01983 613146

Isles of Scilly
St Martin's on the Isle
Lower Town, St Martin's. 01720 422092

Kent
The Hythe Imperial
Hythe. 01303 267441

Kinross-shire
The Green Hotel
2 The Muirs, Kinross. 01577 863467

Lancashire
St. Ives Hotel
St. Anne's on Sea. 01253 720011

Leicestershire
Field Head Hotel
Markfield Lane, Markfield. 01530 245454

London
Charoscuro at Townhouse
24 Coptic Street, WC1. 020 7636 2731

Days Inn Hotel
54 Kennington Road, SE1. 020 7922 1331

London County Hall Travel Inn Capital
Belvedere Road, SE1. 0870 238 3300

myhotel
11-13 Bayley Street, Bedford Square, WC1
020 7667 6040

Norfolk
Heath Farm House B & B
Homersfield, Harleston. 01986 788417

North Devon
Saunton Sands Hotel
Nr Braunton. 01271 890212

Northumberland
Granary Hotel
Links Road, Amble. 01665 710872

Ryecroft Hotel
Ryecroft Way, Wooler. 01668 281459

Perthshire
Gleneagles Hotel
Auchterarder. 0800 328 4010
Playground, crèche

Stronvar House Scottish Vacations
Balquhidder. 01877 384688

Shropshire
Redfern Hotel
Cleobury Mortimer. 01299 270395

South Devon
Gara Rock
East Portlemouth, nr Salcombe. 01548 842342

Suffolk
ICKWORTH HOTEL
Nr Bury St Edmonds. 01284 735350
www.luxuryfamilyhotels.com
East wing of Ickworth House, within 1,800 acre
National Trust estate. Indoor pool and crèche

Visit us at
www.babydirectory.com

Sussex
Family-Friendly Bed & Breakfast
Coombe Barn, Lewes. 01273 477388

Warwickshire
Lea Marston Hotel
Haunch Lane, Lea Marston. 01675 470468

Wiltshire
WOOLLEY GRANGE HOTEL
Woolley Green, Bradford on Avon
01225 864705
www.luxuryfamilyhotels.com
Play area, crèche, outdoor pool, bicycles

Old Bell
Abbey Row, Malmesbury. 01666 822344

Worcestershire
Evesham Hotel
Coopers Lane, Off Waterside, Evesham
01386 765566

Holdfast Cottage Hotel
Welland, Nr Malvern. 01684 310288

hypnotherapy

British Hypnotherapy Association
67 Upper Berkeley Street, London W1
020 7723 4443

ice rinks

Herts

Hemel Hempstead
Silver Blades
Jarman Park. 01442 292202

Berkshire

Slough Ice Arena
Montem Lane. 01753 821555

London

Alexandra Palace Ice Rinks
Alexandra Palace Way, Wood Green, N22
020 8365 2121

Lea Valley Ice Centre
Lea Bridge Road, E10. 020 8533 3155

indoor adventure playcentres

(see also pubs with playgrounds or playrooms)

Herts

Berkhamsted
Kidzone Adventure Playground
Northbridge Road
01442 878441
Up to 11yrs

Bishops Stortford
Adventure Island Playbarn
Parsonage Lane, Sawbridgeworth
01279 600907
1-9yrs

Rascals Ltd
Unit 3 Birchanger Industrial Estate,
Stanstead Road
01279 755771
Toddlers-12yrs

Broxbourne
Toddler World
Lee Valley Leisure Pool, New Nazeing Road
01992 467899
Under 6yrs

Bushey
Activity World
21 Lincolnsfield Centre
01923 233841
Next to Animal Encounter

Hatfield
Activity World
Birchwood Leisure Centre, Longmead
01707 270789

indoor adventure playcentres (cont.)

Hemel Hempstead
Toddler World
Leisure World, Jarman Park
01442 212901

Letchworth
Tumble Tent
The Wynd
01462 627729

London Colney
Adventure World
London Colney Recreation Centre,
Perham Way
01727 822447
up to 11yrs

St Albans
Castaway Kids
156 St Albans Road, Sandridge
01727 844991

South Oxhey
Mini Movers
The Centre, Gosforth Lane
020 8428 4954
Tue-Fri, 1-5yrs, 1-2.30pm

Watford
Action Kid
Unit C, Greatham Road Ind Estate,
Greatham Road
01923 818281

Play Dome
Woodside Retail Park
01923 894801
Parent and toddler mornings 9.30-11.30am
term times

Middx

Brentford
Little Tikes
Brentford Fountain Leisure Centre,
Chiswick High Road
020 8994 9596
Tue-Thur 2-5pm

Snakes and Ladders
Syon Park
020 8847 0946

Greenford
The Ballot Box
Horsenden Lane North, Horsenden Hill
020 8902 2825
Wacky Warehouse

Myllet Arms Hotel
Western Avenue
020 8997 4624
Wacky Warehouse

Harrow
Adventure World
Harrow Leisure Centre, Christchurch Avenue
020 8861 3663

Wembley
Fantasy Island
Vale Farm, Watford Road
020 8904 9044

West Drayton
Sharkeys Fun Factory
3-4 Trout Road, Yiewsley
01895 469046

Bedfordshire

Houghton Regis
The Playground
9 Blackburn Road
01582 660111

Buckinghamshire

Beaconsfield
Zoom
Station Road. 01494 673005

infertility

CHILD - National Infertility Support Network
01424 732361

Foresight
01438 427839
Pre-conceptional nutition to help overcome infertility

Human Fertilisation and Embryology Authority
Paxton House, 30 Artillery Lane, London, E1
020 7377 5077

internet

(see also web sites)

Try your local library – many offer terminals, with easy buggy access. Don't forget to look us up on **www.babydirectory.com**

ironing services

Hillingdon
Pressing Times
01895 437437

Hitchin
Premier Ironing
01438 821182

Northwood
Board of Ironing
01923 823377

St Albans
Little Treasures
01727 843471

Stevenage
Busy Bees Ironing Service
01438 722626

italian

Fantabosco
01923 450610
Italian speaking playgroup in Eastcote

knitting

Zaki-do Dah's Hand-Knits
7 Belgravia House, Halkin Place, London, SW1
07808 159211
Beautiful handknitted babywear from newborn to 18 months. Brochure available

left-handedness

Anything Lefthanded
020 8770 3722

legal advice

Your local Citizen's Advice Bureau is a good starting point. The local library reference department may also be able to help

Children's Legal Centre
01206 873820

Education Law Association
01303 211570
For a list of solicitors in your area

Visit us at
www.babydirectory.com

leisure centres

(see also health clubs with crèches, swimming pools)

May offer toddler gym classes, football, antenatal exercise classes, holiday activities and crèche facilities. Ring for details

Herts

Barnet
Queen Elizabeth Centre
Meadway, Barnet
020 8441 2933

Berkhamsted
Berkhamsted Sports Centre
Lagley Meadow, Douglas Gardens
01442 228123

Borehamwood
The Venue
Potters Lane
020 8386 9886

Bushey
Bushey Grove Leisure Centre
Aldenham Road
01923 470140

Cheshunt
Grundy Park Leisure Centre
Windmill Lane. 01992 623345 (enquiries)

Harpenden
Harpenden Sports Centre
Rothamsted Park, Leyton Road, Harpenden
01582 767722. 01582 460683 (pool)

Hatfield
Birchwood Leisure Centre
Longmead
01707 270772

Hatfield Leisure Centre
Travellers Lane
01707 268769

Hemel Hempstead
Hemel Hempstead Sports Centre
Park Road
01442 228188

Hoddesdon
John Warner Sports Centre
Stanstead Road
01992 445375

Letchworth
North Herts Leisure Centre
Baldock Road
01462 679311

London Colney
London Colney Recreation Centre
Perham Way
01727 822447

Potters Bar
FURZEFIELD CENTRE
Mutton Lane
01707 850500
www.hertsmere.gov.uk/furzefield
Swimming pool, crèche, toddler gym sessions, ante and postnatal exercise classes

Redbourn
Redbourn Recreation Centre
75 Dunstable Road
01582 626202

Rickmansworth
William Penn Leisure Centre
Shepherds Lane, Mill End
01923 771050

St Albans
Bricket Wood Sports Centre
Smug Oak Lane, Bricket Wood
01923 662224

Westminster Lodge Leisure Centre
Holywell Hill
01727 846031

Stevenage
Stevenage Arts & Leisure Centre
Lytton Way
01438 242877

Tring
Tring Sports Centre
Mortimer Hill
01442 228957

Waltham Abbey
Waltham Abbey Sports Centre
Broomstickhall Road
01992 716194

Ware
Wodson Park Sports & Recreation Centre
Wadesmill Road
01920 487091

Watford
The Everett Centre
Leggatts Way. 01923 441444

Watford Leisure Centre
Horseshoe Lane
01923 670644

Welwyn Garden City
Gosling Sports Centre
Stanborough Road
01707 331056

Middx

Edgware
Canon Sports Centre
North London Collegiate School,
Dalkeith Grove
020 8951 5402

Feltham
Feltham Airparcs Leisure Centre
Uxbridge Road, Hanworth
020 8894 9156

Greenford
Greenford Sports Centre
Ruislip Road
020 8575 9157

Harefield
John Penrose Sports Centre
Northwood Way
01895 822929 (eves & weekends)

Harrow
Harrow Leisure Centre
Christchurch Avenue
020 8901 5980

leisure centres (cont.)

Hayes
Harlington Sports Centre
Pinkwell Lane
020 8569 3211

Hayes Stadium Sports Centre
Judge Heath Lane
020 8573 0093

Isleworth
Isleworth Recreation Centre
Twickenham Road
020 8560 6855

Northolt
Compton Leisure Centre
Bengarth Road
020 8841 0953

Northwood
Northwood Sports Centre
Potter Street
01923 824833 (eves & weekends)

Ruislip
Queensmead Sports Centre
Victoria Road
0208 845 6010

Southall
Dormers Wells Leisure Centre
Dormers Wells Lane
020 8571 7207

libraries

(see also toy libraries)

You and your children can join local libraries free of charge on proof of residence and borrow books, videos and cassettes. A fantastic resource, libraries are also a good source of local information. Days and times refer to under 5 storytime sessions. Some libraries run additional activity classes in the school holidays

Barnet

Burnt Oak Library
Watling Avenue, Edgware. 020 8959 3112
Thur 2.30pm

Chipping Barnet Library
3 Stapylton, Barnet
020 8359 4040
Sat 11-11.30am, Wed 2.30-3pm

East Barnet Library
85 Brookhill Road
020 8440 4376
Fri 11-11.30am, Wed 2.15-2.45 (all year),
Sat 11.30-12noon (term times)

Edgware Library
Hale Lane
020 8359 2626
Tue 2.15-2.45pm

Herts Library Service

Days and times refer to storytimes for under 5s. You are advised to phone beforehand to check. Please telephone the Customer Service Centre on the following numbers

	From area codes 01923 or 020	From the rest of Herts
Enquiries	01923 471333	01438 737333
Renewals	01923 471373	01438 737373
Minicom	01923 471599	01438 737599

www.
BABY
directory.com
Lots of Local Up-dates

Abbots Langley Library
High Street
Tue 2.15-2.45pm

Adeyfield Library
1a Queen's Square, Hemel Hempstead

Ashwell Library
Merchant Taylors School, Mill Street
Sat 11.00-11.20am

Baldock Library
Simpson Drive
Fri 2.30-3.00pm

Berkhamsted Library
Kings Road
Thu 2.15-2.45pm

Bishops Stortford Library
The Causeway
Tue 2.00-2.30pm

Borehamwood Library
Elstree Way
Wed 2.15-2.45pm

Bovingdon Library
High Street
Thu 2.30-3.00pm (term-time only)

Brookmans Park Library
Bradmore Green

Buntingford Library
77 High Street
Fri 2.15-2.45pm

Bushey Library
Sparrows Herne
Mon 2.15-2.45pm

Cheshunt Library
Turners Hill
Wed 2.15-2.45
Baby rhyme time, last Tue in month
11-11.30am

Chorleywood Library
Lower Road
Tue 2.15-2.45pm

Cranborne Library
Mutton Lane, Potters Bar
Fri 2.15-2.45pm

Croxley Green Library
Barton Way
Fri 2.15-2.45pm

Cuffley Library
Maynards Place, Station Road
Wed 2.15-2.45pm

Cunningham Library
207 Cell Barnes Lane, St Albans
Tue 2.15-2.45pm (school holidays only)

Fleetville Library
237 Hatfield Road, St Albans
Thu 2.15-2.45pm (term-time only)

Goffs Oak Library
Goffs Lane
Fri 2.00-2.30pm

Harpenden Library
Vaughan Road
Tue 2.15-2.45pm (term-time only)

Hatfield Library
Queensway
Wed 2.00-2.30pm

Hemel Hempstead Library
Combe Street
Tue 2.15-2.45pm

Hertford Library
Old Cross
Tue 10.00-10.30am; Fri 2.00-2.30pm

Hitchin Library
Paynes Park
Tue 2.15-2.45pm

Hoddesdon Library
98a High Street
Tue 2.00-2.30pm

Jackmans Library
Ivel Court, Radburn Way, Letchworth

libraries (cont.)

Kings Langley Library
The Nap
Tue 11.15-11.45am (term-time only)

Knebworth Library
7 St Martins Road
Thu 2.30-3.00pm (term-time only)

Letchworth Library
Broadway
Thu 2.15-2.45pm

Leverstock Green Library
Village Centre, Leverstock Green Road

London Colney Library
Community Centre, Caledon Road

Marshalswick Library
The Ridgeway, St Albans
Tue 2.15-2.45

North Watford Library
St Albans Road, Watford
Tue 2.15-2.45pm

Oakmere Library
High Street, Potters Bar
Mon 2.15-2.45pm

Oxhey Library
Bridlington Road
Tue 2.15-2.45pm

Radlett Library
Aldenham Avenue
Fri 2.15-2.45pm

Redbourn Library
Lamb Lane
Tue 2.30-3.00pm (term-time only)

Rickmansworth Library
High Street
Mon 2.15-2.45pm

Royston Library
Market Hill
Fri 2.00-2.30pm

Sawbridgeworth Library
The Forebury
Wed 2.15-2.45pm

St Albans Central Library
The Maltings
Tue 2.15-2.45pm

Stevenage Library
Southgate
Thu 2.00-2.30pm (term-time only)

Stevenage Old Town Library
38 High Street
Tue 2.15-2.45pm (term-time only)

Tring Library
High Street
Mon 2.30-3.00pm (term-time only)

Waltham Cross Library
123 High Street
Mon 2.15-2.45pm

Ware Library
87 High Street
Fri 2.15-2.45pm

Watford Central Library
Hempstead Road
Tue 2.15-2.45pm

Welwyn Library
Civic Centre, Prospect Place
Mon 2.15-2.45pm (school holidays only)

Welwyn Garden City Central Library
Campus West
Fri 2.15-2.45pm

Wheathampstead Library
Memorial Hall, Marford Road
Thu 2.30-3.00pm (term-time only)

Woodhall Library
Cole Green Lane, Welwyn Garden City
Tue 2.15-2.45pm

Middx

Barham Park Library
Harrow Road, Wembley. 020 8937 3550
Wednesday 2.15-2.45pm

Brentford Library
Boston Manor Road. 020 8560 8801
Thu 2.30pm

Bullsmoor Library
Kempe Road, Enfield. 020 8379 1723

Bush Hill Park Library
Agricola Place, Bush Hill Park, Enfield
020 8379 1709

Ealing Road Library
Ealing Road, Wembley. 020 8937 3560
Mon 2.15-2.45pm

Eastcote Library
88 Field End Road. 0208 866 3688

Enfield Central Library
Cecil Road. 020 8379 8366
Fri 10-11.30am coffee & biscuits 20p
First stop information point 020 8379 8341

Enfield Highway Library
258 Hertford Road. 020 8379 1710
Thu 1.30-2.30pm ((term-time only)

Gayton Library
Gayton Road. 0208 427 8986
Tue 2.15pm

Greenford Library
25 Oldfield Lane South. 020 8578 1466

Harefield Library
Park Lane. 01895 822171

Harlington Library
Pinkwell Lane. 020 8569 1612

Hatch End Library
The Arts Centre, Uxbridge Road, Hatch End,
Pinner. 020 8428 2363
Thu 2.15pm

Hayes End Library
1346 Uxbridge Road. 020 573 4209

Hayes Library
Golden Crescent. 020 8573 2855
Fortnightly Tue

Ickenham Library
Long Lane. 01895 635945

Jublilee Gardens Library
Jubilee Gardens, Southall. 020 8578 1067

Kenton Library
Kenton Lane, Harrow. 020 8907 2463
Tue 2.30pm

Kingsbury Library
Stag Lane. 0208 937 3520
Mon 2.15-2.45pm

Kingshill Library
Bury Avenue, Hayes. 020 8845 3773
Mon fortnightly

Merryhills Library
Enfield Road, Enfield. 020 8379 1711

North Harrow Library
Pinner Road. 020 8427 0677
Thu 2.15pm

Northolt Library
Church Road. 020 8845 3380

Northwood Hills Library
Potter Street. 01923 824595
Alternate Mons 2.15-2.45

Oak Farm Library
Sutton Court Road, Hillingdon. 01895 234690

Oaklands Gate Library
Green Lane, Northwood. 01923 826690
Alternate Thu 2.15-2.45pm

Ordnance Road Library
645 Hertford Road, Enfield. 020 8379 1725
Thu 2.15-3pm

Perivale Library
Horsenden Lane South. 020 8997 2830

Pinner Library
Marsh Road. 020 8866 7827
Thu 2.30pm

Ponders End Library
College Court, High Street. 020 8379 1712
Tue 2.15-3pm, term times

Preston Library
Carlton Avenue East, Wembley. 020 8937 3510
Tue 2.30-3pm

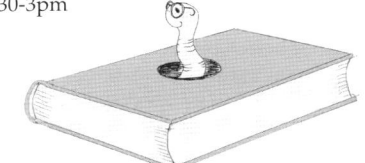

libraries (cont.)

Rayners Lane Library
Imperial Drive. 020 8866 9185
Tue 2.15pm

Roxeth Library
Northolt Road. 020 8422 0809
Thu 2.30pm

Ruislip Library
Bury Street. 01895 633651
Alternate Sats 10.30am (term-time only)

Ruislip Manor Library
Victoria Road. 01895 633668
Alternate Tue 2.15pm

Stanmore Library
8 Stanmore Hill. 020 8954 9955
Thu 2.30pm

Southall Library
Osterley Park Road. 020 8574 3412

South Ruislip Library
Victoria Road. 0208 845 0188
Alternate Tue 2.15pm

Tokyngton Library
Monks Park, Tokyngton. 020 8937 3590
Sat 11.15-12noon

Uxbridge Central Library
High Street. 01895 250600
Fortnightly Fridays 11-12noon

Wealdstone Library
Grant Road. 0208 427 8670
Thu 2.15pm

Wembley Town Hall Library
Town Hall, Forty Lane. 020 8937 3500
Mon 2.15-2.45pm

West Drayton Library
Station Road. 01895 443238

Wood End Library
Whitton Avenue West. 020 8422 3965

Yeading Library
Yeading Lane, Hayes 020 8573 0261

Yiewsley Library
High Street. 01895 442539

lice

NATURAL SCIENCE.COM
Lindslade House, Middleton Street,
Llandrindod Wells, Powys. 01597 823964
lucyabear@btconnect.com
www.lice.co.uk
Nice'n Clear Head Lice lotion - safe, effective,
10 minutes per application

linens

(see also sleeping bags)

COTTON FLEECE BLANKETS
Hippychick Ltd, Barford Gables,
Spaxton, Somerset. 01278 671461
sales@hippychickltd.co.uk
www.hippychickltd.co.uk
100% natural cotton fleece baby blankets in a
wonderful array of colours

THE NURSERY COMPANY
5 Cloncurry Street, London, SW6
020 8878 5167
www.nurserycompany.co.uk
Quality cotton nightwear for ages 2-12 years.
Baby sleeping bags from birth - 3 years

babybabycompany
020 8876 3153

Visit us at
www.babydirectory.com

Subscribe to your local Families Magazine

London area:

Families South West

Families South East

Families North

Families North West

Families West

Families Upon Thames

Families East

Elsewhere:

Thames Valley

Families Edinburgh

Families Liverpool

Ask for a free sample.

Families newsletters are packed full of local info: (new shops, new services, new playgroups, etc), features (parties, nurseries, etc) plus a fantastic Out & About listing.

Written by mothers who have lived in the area for years.

editor@FamiliesMagazine.co.uk for information or to ask about **franchise** *opportunities.* *020 8696 9680*

Send £15.50 payable to Families, PO Box 4302, SW16 1ZS, stating which edition you require.
Also available free in after-school clubs, nurseries and elsewhere.

Online parenting: **www.FamiliesMagazine.co.uk** over a million hits a month!

---

magazines

Families North West
020 8810 5388

Please say you saw the ad in
The Local Baby Directory

Local up-dates on-line

mail order

(*see also aromatherapy, carriers, fancy dress, gifts, linens, maternity wear, organic, sleeping bags*)

mail order: accessories

GOO-GOO
07002 466 466
direct@goo-goo.com
www.goo-goo.com
Functional children's accessories, *see shoes, clothing, mail order: clothing*

BONNE NUIT
020 8871 1472
sales@bonne-nuit.co.uk
www.bonne-nuit.co.uk
Beautiful French baby sleeping bags available in 3 sizes (0-4 years). Winter & summer collection. Call for brochure or stockist, or order online

www.pottypaper.com
Potty training starter kit

mail order (cont.)

mail order: baby goods

GREAT LITTLE TRADING COMPANY
124 Walcot Street, Bath. 0870 2414081
cat@gltc.co.uk
www.gltc.co.uk
Hundreds of practical products designed to
make your life as a parent a little bit easier

www.smilechild.co.uk
PO Box 274, Cheltenham,
Gloucester GL53 7YP. 0800 1956 982
info@smilechild.co.uk
www.smilechild.co.uk
Funky fashion, wooden toys, natural
cosmetics, organics, eco-nappies and more

Mothercare Direct
01923 240365

The Nursery Emporium plc
Grower Court, New Road, Bromham,
Chippenham, Wiltshire. 01380 859171

mail order: clothing

GOO-GOO
07002 466 466
direct@goo-goo.com
www.goo-goo.com
Cocoon - new-born superfine and supersoft
merino wool garments. Machine washable of
course!

JOJO MAMAN BEBE
0870 241 0560
www.jojomamanbebe.co.uk
Great maternity wear, adorable baby &
children's clothes, nursery products & toys -
we're all you need

Silkstory
3 National Terrace, Bermondsey Wall East,
London. 0800 150874

mail order: gifts

Little Angel
01473 323146
www.littleangel.info
A beautiful keepsake box, contains a gift for
mum, dad, baby and can include a gift for
siblings. Starts at £45.00. Brands include Petit
Bateau/Dior

mail order: nursery furniture

DRAGONS OF WALTON STREET
020 7589 3795
Hand-painted children's furniture

House of Winkle
Offa House, Offa Street, Hereford
01432 268018
Organic mattresses & bedding

mail order: shoes

BOBUX
07002 466466
www.goo-goo.com
direct@goo-goo.com
Original soft leather shoes for under twos with
stayonability!

SHOO SHOOS
Hippychick Ltd, Barford Gables,
Spaxton, Somerset. 01278 671461
sales@hippychickltd.co.uk
www.hippychickltd.co.uk
Imaginative and refreshingly different, soft
leather baby shoes (0-24 months)

SOLE MANIA
07002 466466
www.goo-goo.com
direct@goo-goo.com
Durable washable leather slippers for
unstoppable nippers aged 2ish to 90ish

Starchild Shoes
109 Paget Street, Loughborough, Leics
01509 550714
janet@star-child.co.uk
www.star-child.co.uk
Soft leather babies' shoes that really do stay
on…

Visit us at
www.babydirectory.com

mail order: toys

Insect Lore Europe
PO Box 1420, Kiln Farm, Bucks. 01908 563338
Butterfly kits and other equipment

Mulberry Bush Ltd
Freepost SEA 4193, Billingshurst, West Sussex
01403 754400

Worbey Know How Enterprises
07855 080456

manufacturers & suppliers

Baby Dan UK
Nilebank Offices, 10 Beach Priory Gardens,
Birkdale, Southport, Lancashire. 01704 502575

BabyBjorn AB
31-33 Park Royal Road. 0870 1200 543

Bambino Mio Ltd
12 Stavely Way, Brixworth, Northampton
01604 883777

Bebe Confort
Dyehouse Lane, Brighouse, West Yorkshire
01484 401802

Bebecar (UK) Ltd.
Bebecar House, Mill Hill Industrial Estate,
Flower Lane, Mill Hill. 020 8201 0505

Brevi (Trend Europa Ltd.)
Unit D3, Rosehill Industrial Estate, Tern Hill,
Shropshire. 01630 638978

Brio Wonderland Ltd.
4 Nicholas Court, Nicholas Street Mews,
Chester. 01706 750853

Please say you saw the ad in
The Local Baby Directory

manufacturers & suppliers (cont.)

Cheeky Rascals
The Briars, Petworth Road, Witley, Surrey
01428 682489

Chicco UK Ltd.
Prospect Close, Kirkby-in-Ashfield, Notts
01623 750870

Cosatto (sales) Ltd.
Wollaston Way, Burnt Mills, Basildon, Essex
01268 722800

Fisher Price Nursery Products
Maclaren Limited, Station Works,
 Long Buckby, Northampton. 01327 842662

Galt Toys Ltd.
Brookfield Road, Cheadle, Cheshire
0161 428 9111

Graco Children's Products Ltd.
1 Hoverfields Avenue, Burnt Mills Industrial
Estate, Basildon, Essex. 0870 909 0510

Jackel International Ltd.
Dudley Lane, Cramlington, Northumberland
0191 250 1864

Mamas & Papas Ltd.
Colne Bridge Road, Huddersfield,
West Yorkshire. 01484 438200

Maxi-Cosi UK
Isopad House, Shenley Road, Borehamwood,
Herts. 020 8236 0707

Silver Cross Ltd.
Otley Road, Guiseley, Leeds. 01943 876177

Stokke UK Ltd.
154 High Street, West Drayton, Middlesex
01753 655873

Tomy UK Ltd.
Wells House, 231 High Street, Sutton, Surrey
020 8661 4400

Visit us at
www.babydirectory.com

martial arts

(see also leisure centres)

Premier Taekwondo
Eastcote Methodist Church, Pamela Gardens
020 8866 1734
from 4/5yrs

massage for baby & mother

(see also complementary health)

www.thebabyswebsite.com
For a list of baby massage teachers

Bishops Stortford
Isla Ball
01279 813413

Chalfont St Giles
Chris Gallagher
01753 883237

Edgware
Jyoti Gudka
020 8952 5965
See advert under yoga

Harrow
Waldron Studios
020 8423 7635

Hatfield
Birth Works
01707 880333

Hitchin
Hitchin Natural Therapy Centre
3-4 High Street
01462 459020
Pregnancy massage & baby massage

Hoddesdon
Lara O'Kelly
01992 467998

Royston
Billie France
01763 262683

St Albans

Helen Nuttall
01727 848575
Also cranio-sacral therapy

Julie Thomas
07779 032166

Melissa Savage
01727 854627

Stanmore

Middlesex School of Complementary Medicine
Victoria House, 18 Dalston Gardens
020 8204 4441

Tring & Wendover

Louise Page
01296 696285
Pregnancy and baby massage classes

maternity nannies & nurses

(see also doulas, midwives, nanny agencies)

TINIES CHILDCARE
0800 783 6070
info@tinieschildcare.co.uk
www.tinieschildcare.co.uk
Most progressive agency with more nannies, maternity nurses, part-time & emergency carers
See advert under nanny agencies

maternity wear: mail order

BLOOMING MARVELLOUS
020 8391 4822
www.bloomingmarvellous.co.uk

MATERNUS/FORTY WEEKS
020 8299 6761
www.maternus.co.uk
A funky range of maternity basics designed to fit throughout pregnancy

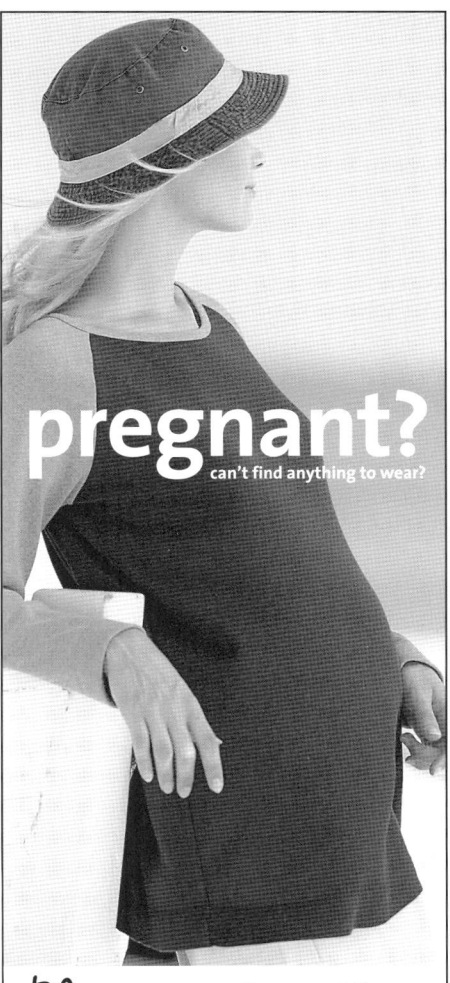

maternity wear: mail order (cont.)

Bumpstart
020 8879 3467

Business Bump
01625 599022

Formes
020 8689 1133

NCT (Maternity Sales) Ltd
239 Shawbridge Street, Glasgow
0141 636 0600

maternity wear: retail & hire

Mothercare branches in most high streets

The Maternity Wear Exchange
01628 851187
www.maternityexchange.co.uk
Second hand for sale or hire

Barnet
Marvellous Seconds
3 Mount Parade, Cockfosters
020 8441 5582

Great Missenden
The Waiting Room
75 High Street
01494 866189
Maternity & baby wear

St Albans
Blooming Marvellous
12 Market Place
01727 836777
See advert on page 55

mathematics

KUMON EDUCATIONAL
www.kumon.co.uk
0800 854714

midwives: independent

Independent Midwives' Association
01483 821104
www.independentmidwives.org.uk

STEPHIE SHEPHERD
01727 753491
www.independent-midwife.co.uk
One to one care – your body, your baby, your choices
See advert on page 57

Jane Dutton
01707 886619
www.homebirths.net

Jane Evans - Independant Midwife
01582 769408

Laura Abbott
01438 833523

Thames Valley Independent Midwives
01753 841873

model agencies

Harrow
ELISABETH SMITH (MODEL AGENCY) LTD
020 8863 2331
models@elisabethsmith.com
www.elisabethsmith.com
Established in 1960 specializing in babies/children/teenagers/families

Berkhamsted
MOT
01442 863918

Visit us at
www.babydirectory.com

mother & baby groups

These are usually for mothers with small babies (pre-crawling) and are often run by the local clinic. The National Childbirth Trust runs groups in people's homes in some areas *(see postnatal support and information)*. Other useful sources of information are Health Visitors, clinics and your local library *(qv)*. For older children, *see parent & toddler groups, playgroups*

Watford
Watford Women's Centre
Lower Mall, 20 Charter Place
01923 240964

Please say you saw the ad in
The Local Baby Directory

murals & painted nursery furniture

(see also nursery furniture & decor, nursery goods)

Beau Reve
01923 499467
www.beaureve.com

Jane Blundell
01462 633574
Murals, stencils paint effects and painted
furniture

Lawrence Mathias
020 8424 9394
Murals

Sandman Beds
01923 283598
www.sandmanbeds.com

museums

(see also outings)

Herts

Hertford
Hertford Museum
18 Bull Plain. 01992 582686
Tue-Sat 10-5pm. Admission free

Hitchin
Hitchin Museum
Paynes Park. 01462 434476
Mon-Sat 10-5pm, free, activities for young
children

Letchworth
Letchworth Museum
The Broadway. 01462 685647
Drop in sessions for mother & toddlers 2-5yrs
once a month. Open Mon-Sat 10-5pm, free

London Colney
De Havilland Heritage Museum
Salisbury Hall. 01727 822051
Early aircraft

St Albans
Verulamium Museum
St Michael's Street
01727 751810

Stanstead
House on the Hill Toy Museum
01279 813237
Can be combined with visit to Mountfitchet
Castle (March-Nov)

Stevenage
Stevenage Museum
St Georges Way. 01438 354292

Tring
Walter Rothschild Zoological Museum
Akeman Street. 01442 824181
Victorian stuffed animals e.g. lions, penguins,
walruses and dogs, displayed at child height

Watford
Watford Museum
194 Lower High Street. 01923 232297
Special children's events

Middx

Harrow
Harrow Museum & Heritage Centre
Headstone Manor, Pinner View. 020 8861 2626

Hendon
Royal Air Force Museum
Grahame Park Way. 020 8205 2266
Open every day 10-6pm

Further afield
Beds

Biggleswade
Shuttleworth Collection
Old Warden Aerodrome, Nr Biggleswade.
01767 627288
Historic collection of cars, motocycles and
aircraft. Restaurant & playground. Open all
year

Luton
Stockwood Craft Museum
Farley Hill. 01582 738714
Craft exhibits, gardens, stables with carriages,
toilets, playground. Free admission

Bucks

Aylesbury
Roald Dahl Childrens Gallery
Bucks County Museum, Church Street
01296 331441
Recommended for older children with a
knowledge of the Roald Dahl stories. Busy!

Cambs

Duxford
Imperial War Museum
01223 835000
Aircraft museum, shop and restaurant,
playground

London

Bethnal Green Museum of Childhood
Cambridge Heath Road, E2. 020 8980 2415
Closed Fri. Mon-Sat, 10-5.50pm;
Sun 2.30-5.50pm

British Museum
Great Russell Street, WC1. 020 7323 8000
Mon-Sat 10-5pm; Sun 10-5.30pm

Cuming Museum
155-157 Walworth Road, SE17. 020 7701 1342

Geffrye Museum
Kingsland Road, E2. 020 7739 9893
Tues-Sat 10-5pm, Sun 2-5pm

Gunnersbury Park Museum
Gunnersbury Park, Popes Lane, W3
020 8992 1612
Excellent local museum

Horniman Museum and Gardens
100 London Road, Forest Hill, SE23
020 8699 1872
www.horniman.ac.uk
Picnic Area. Animals, gardens, child-friendly
aquarium. African Masks and Egyptian
Mummies. Baby changing. Free.
Mon-Sat 10.30-5.30pm; Sun 2-5.30pm

Imperial War Museum
Lambeth Road, SE1. 020 7416 5000

Livesey Museum for Children
682 Old Kent Road, Peckham, SE15
020 7639 5604
Under 5s mornings Thursdays 10-12pm

**London International Gallery of Children's
Art**
02 Centre, 255 Finchley Road, NW3
020 8435 0903
www.ligca.org
Gallery exhibiting children's art. Workshops

London Transport Museum
The Piazza, Covent Garden, WC2
020 7565 7299
www.ltmuseum.co.uk
Mon-Sun, 10-6pm

Museum of London
150 London Wall, EC2. 020 7600 3699
www.museumoflondon.org.uk
Mon-Sat, 10-5.50pm; Sun 12-5.50pm

National Army Museum
Royal Hospital Road, SW3. 020 7730 0717
www.national-army-museum.ac.uk

www.
BABY
directory.com
Visit on-line for more ideas

museums (cont.)

National Gallery
Trafalgar Square, WC2. 020 7839 3321
Free. Mon-Sat, 10-6pm; Wed 10-9pm;
Sun 12-6pm. Quizzes, etc

National Maritime Museum
Romney Park Road, Greenwich, SE10
020 8858 4422
www.nmm.sc.uk

Natural History Museum
Cromwell Road, SW7. 020 7942 5000
www.nhm.ac.uk
Mon-Sat, 10-5.50pm; Sun 11-5.50pm

Pollock's Toy Museum
1 Scala Street, W1. 020 7636 3452
www.pollock.cwc.net
Mon-Sat, 10-5pm

Ragged School Museum
46-50 Copperfield Road, E3. 020 8980 6405
www.raggedschooolmuseum.org.uk
Free. Wed + Thurs 10-5, first Sun of each
month 2-5pm. First Sun of month, family
activities.

Royal Air Force Museum
Grahame Park Way, Hendon, NW9
020 8205 2266
Mon-Sun 10-6pm

Science Museum
Exhibition Road, SW7. 020 7942 4998
Mon-Sat 10-6pm; Sun 11-6pm. Wellcome Wing
includes Launch Pad. Imax cinema

Somerset House
Courtauld Institute and Gilbert Gallery, WC2
020 7848 2526
Family trails, fountains, ice rink during winter

Tate Britain
Millbank, SW1. 020 7887 8000
www.tate.org.uk
Mon-Sat 10-5.50pm; Sun 2-5.50pm

Tate Modern
Bankside, SE1. 020 7887 8687
www.tate.org.uk

Victoria and Albert Museum
Cromwell Road, SW7. 020 7942 2000
Children free. Mon-Sat, 10-5.15pm;
Sun, 11-5.15pm

Wallace Collection
Hertford House, Manchester Square, W1
020 7935 0687
www.the-wallace-collection.org.uk
No buggies. Free

music

(see also art, dance, drama)

**NATIONAL FOUNDATION FOR
YOUTH MUSIC**
One America Street, London SE1
020 7902 1060
www.youthmusic.org.uk
Funding and music projects for prenatal babies
- five-year olds

Herts

Various venues
MONKEY MUSIC
01582 766464
www.monkeymusic.co.uk
Action songs and rhymes, music and
movement, fun with percussion and musical
games

HONKY TONKS
01923 857386
Action Songs, Nursery Rhymes, Playing
Musical Instruments, Listening Skills

MUSICAL MINIS
020 8868 0001
www.musical minis.co.uk
The fun time music group for babies and
toddlers

Visit us at
www.babydirectory.com

FIRST STEPS

Babies and toddlers can take their First Steps into music making with the help of Youth Music funding and projects. Parents and early years specialists can also benefit from music training.

To find out more about the programme visit:

www.youthmusic.org.uk
or call 08450 560 560

Funded by the Arts Council of England   **youth music**
national foundation for

Baldock & Royston
Music with Mum
01763 246415

Bishops Stortford
Music Tree
01279 659318
12mths+

Borehamwood
Honky Tonks
01923 857386

Mini Music Makers
The Venue.
020 8386 9886

Buntingford
Musical Minis
01920 831177

Bushey
Honky Tonks
01923 857386

Cheshunt
3:4 Time
01992 623489
For 3-4 year olds

Cuffley & Goffs Oak
Musical Teapots
01707 875306

Please say you saw the ad in
The Local Baby Directory

music (cont.)

Hemel Hempstead
Dacorum Music Centre
01442 214599
Pre school music from $3^{1}/_{2}$ yrs

Mini Music
Leverstock Green
01442 242987

Tempo Tots
01442 232964

Hertford
Musical Minis
01920 831177

Hitchin
Music Makers
01462 459468

North Herts Music School
01462 434052

Hoddesdon
Musical Teapots
01707 875306
18mths-$2^{1}/_{2}$ yrs, music & movement

Letchworth
Musical Minis
01920 831177

Potters Bar
Honky Tonks
01923 857386

Little Explorers
01707 663272

Radlett & Shenley
Honky Tonks
01923 857386

Rickmansworth
Musical Minis
020 8868 0001

Royston & Stevenage
Music with Mum
01462 790741 / 01462 491317

St Albans
Clatterpillar Music
01727 859028

Da Capo
020 8371 0302

First Music
01727 865237

St Albans Music School
Townsend Drive
01727 860941
Dalcroz Eurhythmics 3-5yrs

Sounds Fun
01727 867303 / 01727 847206

Young Music Makers
United Reform Church, Homewood Road &
Sandpit Lane
01727 862749

Stevenage
Music Train
01438 232593

Musical Minis
01920 831177

Stevenage Music Centre
01438 351138

Tring
Music for Kids
Corpus Christi Church Hall
01442 891453

Various venues
Jo Jingles
01494 676575

Ware
Musical Minis
01920 831177

Watford
Musical Minis
Croxley Green
020 8868 0001

Watford School of Music
Nascot Wood Road
01923 225531

Welwyn Garden City
Musical Minis
01920 831177

Music Train
01438 820981

Middx

Various venues
MONKEY MUSIC
01582 766464
www.monkeymusic.co.uk
Action songs and rhymes, music and
movement, fun with percussion and musical
games

Hatch End
MUSICAL MINIS
020 8868 0001
www.musicalminis.co.uk
The fun time music group for babies and
toddlers

Kenton & Pinner
SAY HELLO TO MUSIC
020 8866 4232
Fun musical session for 3-8's: singing,
movement, orchestral instruments & stories

Pinner
MUSIC & SONG
020 8866 3813
UK's leading baby/infant music specialist

Stanmore
ADVENTURES IN MUSIC
020 8958 2417
Nickki Gilbert's popular, stimulating music
groups are held in Stanmore

Eastcote
Music Box
020 8864 6106

Enfield
Rondo
020 8360 5790

Greenford
Annapurna Asian Music School
020 8578 1205

Harrow
GEMS Music Adventure Workshops
020 8864 4022

Music Box
020 8864 6106

Musical Infants
020 8954 7701

Say Hello to Music
020 8866 4232
Classes in Kenton

music (cont.)

Harrow (cont.)
West London YMCA
Victoria Halls, Sheepcote Road
020 8427 8041

Northwood
Let's Make Music
01923 828812
12mths-5yrs

Melodies
54 High Street
01923 827991
Piano lessons from 4yrs

Pinner
Movement & Dance
020 8866 3013

Music & Song
020 8866 3813
UK's leading baby/infant music specialist

Musical Minis
Hatch End
020 8868 0001

Say Hello to Music
020 8866 4232

Southall
Asian Arts & Music Academy
020 8574 1900

Stanmore
Adventures in Music
020 8958 2417

Various venues
Jo Jingles
01494 676575

Wembley Park
Twinkletunes
020 8357 1864
6mths+

name tapes

EASY2NAME
01635 298326
easy2name@aol.com
www.easy2name.com
Easy2name suppliers of dishwasher proof
stickers and iron-on tapes

SIMPLY STUCK
01264 350788
www.simplystuck.com
Innovative personalised name labels. Tested
by thousands of children!

naming ceremonies

(see also registration of births)

Baby Naming Society
Yeoman's Cottage, Kerswell Green, Kempsey,
Worcestershire. 01905 371070

British Humanist Association
47 Theobald's Road, London, WC1
020 7430 0908
National Helpline 0990 168122

Please say you saw the ad in
The Local Baby Directory

nanny agencies

(see also au pair agencies, babysitters, childcare listings magazine, childminders, maternity nannies)

BIZZY NANNIES
39 Mill Way, Rickmansworth
01923 441064
www.bizzy-nannies.co.uk
Bizzy Nannies provide & recruits staff in Hertfordshire, Buckinghamshire & Middlesex

GRAPEVINE NANNIES
Ramla, 21 Shire Lane, Chorleywood
01923 286985
We have Nannies, Mother's Helps, Babysitters & Housekeepers available

MULBERRY NANNY AGENCY
Mulberry House, 30 Devereux Drive, Watford
01923 231069 / 244804
www.mulberry-nannies.co.uk
Leading agency established 1984 covering locally, London and Abroad

REGENCY NANNIES
2 Penta Court, Station Road
020 8420 4401
regencynannies@aol.com
Professional, friendly nanny & Maternity nurses, established 1983. REC member

ROWAN NANNIES
The Rowans, Hollybush Close, Berkhamsted
01442 876846
www.rowanagency.com
Established 1990 providing quality childcare and free friendly advice

SMALL PEOPLE LTD
16 Station Road, Knebworth
01438 813482

TINIES HERTFORDSHIRE
15 Ely Road, St Albans
01727 761476
herts@tinieschildcare.co.uk
www.tinieschildcare.co.uk

nanny agencies (cont.)

TINIES MIDDLESEX
5 Melrose Gardens, Edgware
020 8204 8099
middlesex@tinieschildcare.co.uk
www.tinieschildcare.co.uk

nanny payroll services

(see also financial advice)

NANNYTAX
PO Box 988, Brighton BN2 1BY
01273 626256
mailbox@nannytax.co.uk
www.nannytax.co.uk
Nannytax is the UK's leading payroll service for parents employing a nanny

NANNY PAYROLL SERVICE
Payday Services Ltd, The Studio,
Benefield Road, Brigstock, Kettering,
Northants
01536 373111
www.nannypayroll.co.uk

nappies: cloth & other

GET REAL
01462 636188
Campaigning for real nappies in Herts & Beds. Cotton nappies – they're easier than you think!

ECO BABES
01462 636188
happynappyuk@yahoo.co.uk
For information and friendly advice about cotton washable nappies call Sarah Mailer

Kooshies
31-33 Park Royal Road, London NW10
0870 607 0545
www.thebabycatalogue.com

Lollipop
01923 441716

The UK's leading Payroll Service for Parents & their Nannies

SUBSCRIBE TODAY BY PHONE - ALL MAJOR CREDIT CARDS ACCEPTED

NANNYTAX is *the original* friendly, *inexpensive* payroll service designed to look after all of your legal, payroll and paperwork obligations when employing a nanny. Leading nanny agencies throughout the UK recommend NANNYTAX to their clients. We have several imitators but no equals!

More than just a payroll service, NANNYTAX supports its clients throughout the employment process and has earned an enviable reputation for excellent customer service. Thousands of appreciative parents from every part of the UK subscribe to NANNYTAX.

Call 01273 626256 for an information pack - www.nannytax.co.uk

Moon Mamma
01727 764602
Also reusable sanitary protection

Plush Pants Cloth Nappies
55 Newlands Avenue, Cheadle Hulme,
Cheshire
0161 485 4430
www.plushpants.co.uk

Real Nappy Association
PO Box 3704, London SE26 4RX. 020 8299 4519
Information on all nappy-related issues

Spirit of Nature Ltd
Burrhart House, Cradock Road, Luton
01582 847370
Nappies, unbleached disposables also natural clothing

Nanny Agencies on-line

Please say you saw the ad in
The Local Baby Directory

nappy delivery: hire & laundry

COTTON FRESH NAPPY SERVICE
0800 3285249
www.cottonfresh.co.uk
Cotton nappy laundering service plus
everything you need for baby

National Association of Nappy Service
(NANS)
0121 693 4949
www.changeanappy.co.uk

Cotton Botties Nappy Service
01223 245245
Deliver to Royston & Bishops Stortford

Nappycare
020 8998 8799
Delivers to Greenford / Harrow / Northolt

Number Ones for Nappies
01992 713665
Deliver to Hertford & Middx

nearly new equipment, toy & clothing shops

The Maternity Wear Exchange
01628 851187
www.maternityexchange.co.uk
Maternity clothes

Berkhamsted
Carousel Clothes
01442 872486
Party plan nearly new clothes

Borehamwood
Kute Kids
102 Shenley Road
020 8207 5558

East Barnet
Junior Jungle
18 Church Hill Road
0208 441 2551

Enfield
www.0-10 again.co.uk
020 8366 3583
New and nearly new children's clothes
through website or by home appointment

Feltham
Trading Places
112 The Centre
020 8893 2960

Hertford
Merry-go-round
50 Mandeville Road
01992 584846
Fri 9am-1pm

Hitchin
Nips n Tucks
3 Arcade Walk
01462 453444

Radlett
Swap Shop
165 Watling Street
01923 855822

Redbourne
Little Treasures
19a High Street
01582 794970

Wealdstone
Gear Change
The Little Warehouse, Gordon Road
020 8863 8584

Whaddon, Nr Royston
Nippers
Leyhill Farm, 2 Bridge Street
01223 207071

nurseries: private

(see also helplines: education, nurseries: day, schools, tuition)

There is an overlap in the field of private childcare provision and education, and many of the terms seem to be interchangeable amongst the providers. In the private sector, **Pre-prep schools** (preparing the child for big school at 5 or 7 years old) have been listed under the schools section, though they often have a nursery class for 3- or 4-year-olds, and this section should also be consulted. **Prep school** then takes your child through to 11 or 13 by which time you will have well outgrown this book *(see family planning)*.

Babies from 3 months onwards can attend a **nursery** or **day care nursery**. In many of these nurseries, older children will graduate from the baby section to a more structured section very like a nursery school, but with longer hours for play, sleep, etc. In general, a **crèche** only offers a few hours of unstructured supervision, while parents do something else *(see health clubs with crèches, shopping crèches)*. At a **playgroup** the carer usually remains in attendance. A **nursery school** for $2^1/2$ to 5 year-olds usually follows a basic school day (9am-3.30pm) and term but pupils may attend only one session, morning or afternoon. Many nurseries use **Montessori** methods, a system devised by Maria Montessori in 1907 which emphasises training of the senses and encouragement rather than a rigid academic curriculum.

For nearly all nurseries and schools in the private sector, early registration is recommended, so ring, visit and inform yourself in time, even if you later decide not to pursue that option.

For a list of **state-run** nurseries, or state primary schools with nursery classes attached, contact your Under 8s section at the local council *(see under councils)* or check out www.childcare.gov.uk
Good luck. You'll need it!

nurseries: day

(see also education, schools, tuition)

Day nurseries offer a full days care, which is usually from 8am-6pm, all year round. Some also offer the facility of late pick up or early drop off times. They accept children from either around 3 months or $2^1/2$ years up to school age. Some of these nurseries for older children may offer fewer hours in the day or run termly.

If no age is indicated the nursery offers care from 3 months

Herts

Abbots Langley
Little Poppets Nursery School
10 Katherine Place, College Road
01923 681826

Aldenham
Wall Hall Day Nursery
Wall Hall Campus
01707 285775

Ashwell
Gloria's Day Nursery
35 West End
01462 742219

Baldock
Puddleducks Day Nursery
Butterfield House, Hitchin Street
01462 490955

nurseries: day (cont.)

Berkhamsted
MARLIN CHILD CARE
1 Park View Road
01923 663875

Pooh Corner Day Nursery
Ashlyns School, Chesham Road
01442 863286

Bishops Stortford
Bright Horizons Day Nursery
Turners Crescent, St Michaels Mead
01279 755522

Busy Bees Day Nursery
Thorley Centre, Thorley
01279 654830

Children's Cottage
Pledgdon Close, Henham
01279 850755

Childways Day Nursery
Herts & Essex Hospital, Haymeads Lane
01279 655191
$2^1/_2$yrs+

Saplings Independent Nursery
Birchwood High School, Parsonage Lane
01279 505244

Borehamwood
Cheeky Monkeys Nursery
96 Shenley Road
020 8207 2333
$2^1/_2$yrs+

Summerswood Nursery
Furzehill Road
020 8923 3139
3yrs+

Bovingdon
Old MacDonalds Day Nursery
Darley Ash Farm
01442 834118

Broxbourne
Squirrels Day Nursery
Hertford Regional College, Broxbourne Centre
01992 448593

Buntingford
Buntingford Kindergarten
London Road
01763 273609
$2^1/_2$yrs+

Bushey
Asquith Court Nursery
David Lloyd Club, Hartspring Lane
01923 213758

Baby World
14 Purlings Road
020 8386 5967

Longwood School & Nursery
Aldenham Road, Bushey Hall Drive
01923 253715

Chorleywood
Primrose Cottage Day Nursery
Primrose Cottage, 2 Hillside Road
01923 282920

Gilston
Colourbox Montessori Nursery
Gilston Village Hall, Pye Corner
01279 724029

Goffs Oak
Little Sparrows Day Nursery
St James Hall, St James Road
01707 876298

Harpenden

Asquith Court Nursery
Peel House, 15 Vaughan Road
01582 762981

Busy Bees Day Nursery
Rothamsted Lodge, Hatching Green
01582 462533

Copperbeech Day Nursery
23 Leyton Road
01582 762220

Lynmore Nursery School
34 Sun Lane
01582 764172
$2^{1}/_{2}$yrs+

Hatfield

Hatfield Day Nursery
University of Hertfordshire, College Lane
01707 279000

Tara Kindergarten
The Annexe, Countess Anne School,
School Lane
01707 265965

Hemel Hempstead

JIGSAW DAY NURSERY
Buncefield Lane
01442 211770
hemelhempstead@jigsawgroup.com
www.jigsawgroup.com
Come and see for yourself why we are the best

LIME GROVE DAY NURSERY
(CHILD BASE)
Park Road
01442 236506
limegrove@childbase.com
www.childbase.com
We care as much as you do

Cherry Tree Day Nursery
15 Horselers, Bennetts End
01442 247237

Moor End Farm Kindergarten
London Road, Boxmoor
01442 246437

Playplus Kindergarten Ltd
Kingsway, London Road, Bourne End
01442 862494

nurseries: day (cont.)

St Nicholas Nursery
Bennetts End House, Eastwick Row
01442 253488

Bees Knees Day Nursery
Cambrian Way, Highfield
01442 393341

Hertford
Bonnie Babies
Sovreign House, Hale Road
01992 503255

Busy Bees Day Nursery
Pinder Lodge, Hartham Park
01992 503610

Copperbeech Day Nursery
Hartham Park, Port Hill
01992 503610

Grasshoppers Day Nursery
Leahoe Gardens
01992 556680

Little Sunbeams
22 Baker Street
01992 589020
2 1/2yrs+

Hitchin
Badgers Day Nursery
17 Walsworth Road
01462 420101

Highbury Lodge Day Nursery
11 Highbury Road
01462 434317

Kinders Mill Day Nursery
11 Trevor Road
01462 642666

Smartys
Old Community Centre, Burford Way
01462 441397

Strathmore Daycare
Strathmore School, Old Hale Way
01462 420299
2 1/2-5yrs

Tiggers Day Nursery
North Herts College, Cambridge Road
01462 424318

Hoddesdon
Haslewood & Roselands Nursery
Haslewood Junior School, Haslewood Avenue
01992 303051

Little Angels Day Nursery
Unit 8, Optima Business park, Pindar Road
01992 466138

Letchworth
JIGSAW DAY NURSERY
Icknield Way
01462 683761
letchworth@jigsawgroup.com
www.jigsawgroup.com
Come and see for yourself why we are the best

Wonderland Day Nursery
Works Road
01462 480884

London Colney
First Adventure
Adventure World, Perham Way
01727 822447

Luton
JIGSAW DAY NURSERY
950 Capability Green
01582 450200
luton@jigsawgroup.com
www.jigsawgroup.com
Come and see for yourself why we are the best

Northchurch
Home from Home Kindergarten
Northchurch Cricket club, Dudswell Lane
01442 874461

Potters Bar
Head Start Day Nursery
86 High Street
01707 655122

Visit us at

www.babydirectory.com

Radlett
JIGSAW DAY NURSERY
22 Andrew Close, Shenley
01923 857585
shenley@jigsawgroup.com
www.jigsawgroup.com
Come and see for yourself why we are the best

Redbourn
RAVENSTONE HOUSE
South Common
01582 792060
www.ravenstonehouse.co.uk

Rickmansworth
Little Shepherds Day Nursery
Shepherds JMI School, Shepherds Lane
01923 448505

Royston
Bumpkins
Leyhill Farm, 2 Bridge Street, Whaddon
01223 208777

Orchards Day Nursery
36c Kneesworth Street
01763 241577

Sun Hill Day Nursery
The Mount
01763 226030

Sun Hill Upper Day Nursery
Market Hill
01763 226036
$2^1/_2$yrs+

Sawbridgeworth
Cherish Private Day Nursery
The Elms, Bell Street
01279 600966

St Albans
Albany Montessori School
Methodist Church Hall, 133B Hatfield Road
01727 848411
$2^1/_2$-5yrs

Beechwood Nursery
70 Beechwood Avenue
01727 852104

Brock House Nursery
31 Clarence Road
01727 855330

Busy Bees Day Nursery
52 Bernard Street
01727 860542

Busy Bees Day Nursery
601 Hatfield Road, Smallford
01727 846469

Busy Bees Day Nursery
12 King Harry Lane
01727 854499

Grasshoppers Day Nursery
20 York Road
01727 852097

Home from Home Daycare Nursery
52a Bernard Street
01727 811212

nurseries: day (cont.)

Little Steps
1 Lancaster Road
01727 856651

Oak Tree Nursery
512 Hatfield Road
01727 857521
2^1/$_2$yrs+ term time

Wainscot Nursery
Wainscot House, St Bernard Road
01727 868550

Stevenage
JIGSAW DAY NURSERY
Stevenage Leisure Park, Kingsway
01438 314309
stevenage2@jigsawgroup.com
www.jigsawgroup.com
Come and see for yourself why we are the best

JIGSAW DAY NURSERY
North Herts College, London Road
01438 722563
stevenage@jigsawgroup.com
www.jigsawgroup.com
Come and see for yourself why we are the best

Just Learning Nursery
01732 846333

Linda's Day Nursery
St John's Ambulance Hall, Stanmore Road
01438 315354
2^1/$_2$yrs+

Noah's Ark Day Nursery
Shephall View
01438 749090

Phoenix Nursery
Ridgemond Park, Telford Avenue
01438 352366
2^1/$_2$yrs+

Tring
Ladybird Day Nursery
Tring Park Cricket Club
01442 879608
2yrs+

Ware
Clinton Kiddicare
Clinton Poles Lane, Thundridge
01920 469053

Little Angels Nursery
Sucklings Yard, Church Street
01920 485021

Stepping Stones Day Nursery
38 Crib Street
01920 469698

Woodside Nursery
Station Road, Braughing
01920 821308

Watford
MARLIN CHILD CARE
St Andrews Montessori School,
High Elms Lane, Garston Manor
01923 663875
See advert on page 70

Buffer Bear Day Nursery
Watford Junction Station, Station Road
01923 207065

Cassio Campus Day Nursery
West Herts College, Langley Road
01923 812277

Park Nursery School & Day Nursery
3 Park Avenue
01923 202056

Toad Hall Nursery
100 Hempsted Road
01923 254637

Tots Day Nursery
Leavesden Green School, High Road,
Leavesden
01923 681092
1yr+

Welwyn
Busy Bees Day Nursery
1 Mardley Hill
01438 840238

Please say you saw the ad in
The Local Baby Directory

bringing up baby

With our strong educational programmes and high calibre staff, we offer your child the best start in life.

Day Nursery provision for 3 month to 5 year olds

Quality education and care for your child

Qualified staff to meet all emotional, social and cultural needs

Varied and stimulating curriculum

Safe, welcoming, child friendly premises

Open minimum 50 weeks, 10 hour days

Nurseries in Brentford, Camden, Hammersmith and Wembley

FOR FURTHER INFORMATION:
020 7738 0160
www.bringingupbaby.co.uk
E-mail: office@bringingupbaby.co.uk

INVESTOR IN PEOPLE

nurseries: day (cont.)

Welwyn Garden City
JIGSAW DAY NURSERY
Kestrel Way, Shire Park
01707 393380
shirepark@jigsawgroup.com
www.jigsawgroup.com
Come and see for yourself why we are the best

Oaklands College Day Nursery
Oaklands College, The Campus
01727 737527

Partners Child Care Centre
YMCA, Peartree Lane
01707 351406

Rowan Tree Day Nursery
9 Guessens Road
01707 334715

Squirrels Day Nursery
Oaken Grove
01707 391797
$2^{1}/_{2}$yrs+

Middx

Alperton
Alperton Nursery
c/o Sainsbury's Alperton Store,
360 Ealing Road
020 8566 7663

Bluebell Nursery
50 Carlyon Road
020 8566 7876

Happy Child Nursery
Middlesex House, Northwick Road
020 8998 4949

St James Nursery
St James Church Centre, Stanley Avenue
020 8902 6231
$2^{1}/_{2}$yrs+

Teenies & Tweenies
Perivale Methodist Hall, May Gardens
020 8997 4468
$2^{1}/_{2}$yrs+

Barnet
WOODLANDS NURSERY
(CHILD BASE)
1-3 Orchard Road
020 8447 1914
woodlandsbarnet@childbase.com
www.childbase.com
We care as much as you
See advert on page 71

The Highgate Montessori
Wesley Hall, Stapyleton Road
020 8447 1848

Brentford
BRENTFORD DAY NURSERY
Half Acre
020 8568 7561
www.bringingupbaby.co.uk
See advert on page 75

TEDDIES
The Old School Building, The Ham
020 8847 3799
www.teddiesnurseries.co.uk
See advert on page 79

Buttercups Day Nursery
Cherry Lane School, Sipson Road
01895 431525

Just Kidding Day Care
44 Boston Park Road
020 8568 4447

Ladybird Lane Day Nursery
122 Windmill Road, St Faiths Church Hall
020 8232 8839
$2^{1}/_{2}$yrs+

Burnt Oak
Orange Hill Daycare Nursery
Watling Community Centre,
145 Orange Hill Road
020 8906 8228
$2^{1}/_{2}$yrs+

Visit us at
www.babydirectory.com

Eastcote
4 Street Nursery
Fore Street
01895 623288
2 yrs+

Rosewood Montessori School
Haydon Hall, Joel Street
020 8866 4701
2$^1/_2$-5yrs

Sundew Montessori
St Thomas More's Catholic Church,
32 Field End Road
020 8357 7914
2yrs+

Edgware
Rexton House Nursery School
Whitchurch Institute, Buckingham Road
020 8951 3742
2$^1/_2$yrs+

Enfield
Asquith Court Nursery
51 Glyn Road
020 8805 1144

Asquith Court Nursery
2 Queen Anne's Place, Bush Hill Park
020 8364 1188

Busy Bees
180 Carterhatch Lane
020 8367 0069

Carol Jane Montessori Nursery
80 The Ridgeway
020 8364 4440

Cedar Park Nursery
Wolverton, Hadley Road
020 8367 3800

Cedar Park Nursery
Hymnus House, Browning Road
020 8342 1414
2$^1/_2$yrs

Chace Community School Nursery
Chace School, Churchbury Lane
020 8352 8216

Goldstar Montessori Nursery
466 Baker Street
020 8364 6876
2$^1/_2$yrs+

Stepping Stones Nursery
139 Southbury Road
020 8363 5468
2$^1/_2$yrs+

Tara Kindergarten
198 High Street, Ponders End
020 8804 7710
3mths-5yrs

Feltham
Once upon a Time
Blair Athol house, 7 Ashfield Avenue
020 8751 5810

Greenford
Bright Horizons Day Nursery
Greenford Road
020 8422 0122

Fairytale Day Nursery
Greenford Hall, Ruislip Road
020 8575 6301

Fairytale Day Nursery
Currey Road
020 8423 5577

Sudbury Town Nursery School
Old Odeon Building, Allendale Road
020 8902 4999
2$^1/_2$yrs+

Tops & Tails Day Nursery
364a Whitton Avenue East
020 8900 2063

Year of the Child Day Nursery
55 Eastmead Avenue
020 8813 0147

Harefield
Beehive Nursery
Harefield Hospital, Hill End Road
01895 828898

The Childlink Centre
The Plough, Hill End Road
01895 822129

nurseries: day (cont.)

Harrow
Asquith Court Pre-school & Nursery
9 The Ridgeway, Kenton
020 8909 9850

Granary Pre-School
100 Trescoe Gardens
020 8423 7678
2yrs+

Happy Days Nursery
Sea Cadet Hall, Woodlands Road
020 8424 0102

Learning Tree Montessori Nursery School
309 Preston Road
020 8904 9413
2^1/$_2$yrs+

Pre-School Playhouse
1a Walton Road
020 8424 2157
2^1/$_2$yrs

Teddies Nursery
Northwick Park Hospital
020 8869 3937

Tyneholme Day Nursery
Headstone Drive
020 8863 1168
2^1/$_2$yrs+

Hayes
Cuddles Day Nursery
Christ Church, Waltham Avenue
020 8813 7356

Hayes Early Years Centre
Nestles Avenue
020 8573 0229

Hungry Caterpillars Day Nursery
St Edmunds Church Hall, Edmunds Close
020 8573 5228

Uxbridge College Nursery
Hayes Community Campus,
Coldharbour Lane
01895 853800
2^1/$_2$yrs+

Heathrow
Jigsaw Day Nursery
4 Ironbridge Road, Stockley Park West
020 8573 5723

Wonderland Day Nursery
Holiday Inn
020 8745 1356

Hillingdon
Activity Babies
The Scout Hut, Daleham Drive
01895 436006

Scallywags Nursery
Hillingdon Infants School, Uxbridge Road
01895 239280

TLC
Hillingdon Hospital, Pield Heath Road
01895 270870

New Barnet
Head Start Nursery
54 Station Road
01438 840681

Nightingale Nursery
Park Entrance, 23 Victoria Road
020 8441 8788
2^1/$_2$yrs+

North Harrow
North Harrow Day Nursery
39 Gloucester Road
020 8427 0114

Northolt
Fairy Tale Day Nursery
Northolt Day Centre, Ealing Road
020 8845 5898

Medcliffe Community Nursery
41 Woburn tower, Broomcroft Avenue
020 8841 1289

Mini Kids Montessori Nursery School
St Richards Church Hall
020 8423 8786

Visit us at
www.babydirectory.com

Pride and Joy Day Nursery
Scout Hut, Eskdale Road
020 8842 4244
2¹/₂yrs+

Northwood
RIVERSIDE TEDDIES
Riverside Club, Ducks Hill Road
01923 848041
www.teddiesnurseries.co.uk

Mount Vernon Day Nursery
Mount Vernon Hospital, Rickmansworth Road
01923 844141

Woodlodge Montessori School
Shelley House, 97 Hilliard Road
01923 833472

Perivale
Busy Bees Day Nursery
34-38 Bideford Avenue
020 8810 4207

Happy Child Day Nursery
Hanwell Town Football Club, Perivale Lane
020 8998 6255

Pinner
Asquith Court Pre School & Nursery
3 Hillview Road, Hatch End
020 8421 5471

MARLIN NURSERY SCHOOL
01923 663875
2¹/₂yrs+

Pinner Day Nursery
Buckingham Prep School, 458 Rayners Lane
020 8868 1260
2¹/₂yrs+

St Vincents Day Nursery
St Vincents Hospital, Wiltshire Lane
020 8426 1490

Queensbury
Beverley Lodge Nursery
Queensbury Methodist Church,
Beverley Drive
07949 658 428

Rayners Lane
Pritti Babes Day Nursery
The Venturers Boys Club, Yeading Avenue
020 8866 2929

Ruislip
Activity Two Day Nursery
3 Thurlstone Road
01895 634346

Bright Sparks Montessori School
120 Elliot Avenue, off Southbourne Gardens
01895 672301
2¹/₂yrs+

Growing Tree Nursery
Ruislip RFC, West End Road
01895 622223
2¹/₂yrs+

Happy Child Day Nursery
Dawlish Drive
01895 676355

Highgrove Early Years Centre
31 Campbell Close
01895 638327

nurseries: day (cont.)

Lady Bankes EYE Nursery
Lady Bankes Schools, Dawlish Drive
01895 636765
$2^1/2$yrs+

Ruislip
Little Wings Day Nursery
RAF Northolt, West End Road
020 8842 3518

Once Upon a Time
Cavendish Pavilion, Field End Road
020 8906 8076
18mths+

Pre-School Playhouse
Ruislip Gardens Infants School, Stafford Road
01895 624454

White House Nursery
97 West End Road
01895 632681

Woodlands Nursery
Woodford Hall, Poplars Close
01895 622140
$2^1/2$yrs+

Ruislip Gardens
Eilmar Montessori School & Day Nursery
Sidmouth Drive
0800 980 9919
$2^1/2$yrs+

South Ruislip
South Ruislip Early Years Centre
Station Approach
020 8845 6669

Southall
Toad Hall Nursery
Corner Crescent, off Windmill Avenue
020 8571 6867

Year of the Child Day Nursery
100 Carlyle Avenue
020 8571 6378
$2^1/2$yrs+

Uxbridge
Activity One Nursery
Scout Hall, Gatting Way
01895 274206
$2^1/2$yrs+

Buffer Bear Nursery
Inglenook, Sipson Lane, Sipson
020 8759 5457

Once upon a Time Day Nursery
Friends Meeting House, 150 York Road
01895 256335

Once upon a Time Day Nursery
Rockingham Road
01895 255479
$2^1/2$yrs+

Premier Nursery & Montessori
St John's Road
01895 234455
3mths-5yrs

Tara Kindergarten
Lawn Road
01895 273133

Uxbridge Early Years Centre
57 Park Road
01895 232539

Young Fliers Day Nursery
501 Bath Road, Heathrow Airport
01753 686029

Wembley
VALE DAY NURSERY
Wembley Football Club, Vale Farm, Watford Road
020 8385 1928
www.bringingupbaby.co.uk
See advert on page 75

Barnhill Nursery
Barnhill Road
020 8908 3028

College of North West London Nursery
140 Wembley Park Drive
020 8208 5224

Douglas Avenue Nursery
Douglas Avenue
020 8903 7254

Honeypot Nursery
Ujima House, 388 High Road
020 8903 9367

London Road Nursery
Patidar House, 22 London Road
020 8795 1648
2$^1/_2$yrs+

Mulberry Tree Nursery
Truscott Hall, Wembley Hill Road,
Empire Way
020 8902 0654
2$^1/_2$yrs+

Parklands Kindergarten
Northwick Park Sports Pavilion, The Fairway
020 8385 2005
2$^1/_2$yrs+

Stepping Stones Nursery
Vale Farm Sports & Leisure Centre,
Watford Road
020 8904 8546
2$^1/_2$yrs+

Sunflower Day Nursery
Wembley Park sports & Social Club,
Forty Avenue
020 8908 6712
2$^1/_2$yrs+

Windermere Nursery
Church of the Annunciation,
Windermere Avenue
020 8904 3327
2$^1/_2$yrs+

West Drayton
Asquith Court Nursery
The Old Vicarage, High Street,
Harmondsworth
020 8754 0659

Premier Nursery
Trout Road, Yiewsley
01895 444449

Winchmore Hill
WOODBERRY (CHILD BASE)
63 Church Hill, London N21 1LE
020 8882 6917
Woodberry@childbase.com
www.childbase.com
We care as much as you
See advert on page 71

nursery furniture & decor

(see also mail order: furniture, murals & painted nursery furniture, nursery goods)

LIONWITCHWARDROBE
020 8265 8449
info@lionwitchwardrobe.co.uk
www.lionwitchwardrobe.co.uk
Hand-crafted contemporary oak furniture and
accessories for style-conscious parents

Ragazzi Nursery Furniture
01993 774601
www.ragazzi.com

The Children's Furniture Company
020 7737 7303
www.thechildrensfurniturecompany.com

nursery goods

(see also clothing shops, mail order)

Herts

Barnet
Junior Jungle
18 Church Hill Road, East Barnet
020 8441 2551

Mothercare
129 High Street
020 8449 0080

Berkhamsted
Classie Chassis
29-33 Lower Kings Road
01442 864252

nursery goods (cont.)

Bishops Stortford
Baby Bits
Jackson Square
01279 653300

Borehamwood
Kindercare
130 Shenley Road
020 8953 7701

Cheshunt
Mothercare
Unit 1 Halfhide Lane
01992 636625

Hatfield
Kid Kraft
92 The Galleria
01707 273020

Hemel Hempstead
Hansell & Grettal
23 Bennetts Gate, Bennetts End
01442 252633

Mothercare
34a Marlowes Center
01442 252860

Letchworth
Mothercare
13 Eastcheap
01462 684067

Scruples
45 Leys Avenue
01462 685911

Royston
Nippers
Leyhill Farm, 2 Bridge Street, Whaddon
01223 207071

Stevenage
Mothercare
BHS, 7 The Forum
01438 742292

Mothercare World
Monkswood Retail Park
01438 750211

Ware
Bush Babes
The Maltings
01920 484555

Watford
John Lewis
The Harlequin
01923 244266

Mothercare World
Watford Arches Retail Park
01923 246093

Welwyn Garden City
John Lewis
Bridge Road
01707 323456

Mothercare
Unit 20 Howard Centre
01707 373640

Middx

Little Stars
020 8621 4378 or 8537 0980
www.littlestars.co.uk

Ealing
Daniel Baby Centre
96-122 Uxbridge Road
020 8567 6789

Edgware
Young Smartees
144 Burnt Oak Broadway
020 8952 7796

Enfield
Mothercare
4-6 Palace Gardens
020 367 1188

The Pram Centre
12 Savoy Parade, Southbury Road
020 8367 2512

Tiny Tots
236 Hertford Road
020 8804 1946

Visit us at
www.babydirectory.com

Harrow
Graham's Toys
178-180 Alexandra Avenue, South Harrow
020 8422 2610

Mothercare
80-82 St Anns Road
020 8427 2349

Simply Baby
Northwick Park Hospital, Watford Road
020 8864 7584

Hayes
Mothercare World
Lombardy Retail Park, Coldharbour Lane
020 8561 6011

Northwood Hills
Mini Modes
1-3 Joel Street
01923 826935

Ruislip Gardens
Baby Boom 2000
4 New Pond Parade, West End Road
01895 675596

nutrition

www.zitawest.com
0870 668899

Johanna Scarry
020 8909 2603

British Dietetic Association
0121 200 8080

Foresight: Association for Preconceptual Care
01483 427839

Waldron Studios
Holistic Education Centre, Waldron Road,
Harrow
020 8423 7635

Wellbeing Eating for Pregnancy Helpline
0114 242 4084

organic

(see also food, nappies: cloth & other)

Schmidt Natural Clothing
01342 822169
www.natural clothing.co.uk

Green Baby
345 Upper Street, London, N1
020 7226 4345
www.greenbabyco.com

Little Green Earthlets
01825 873301
www.earthlets.co.uk

osteopaths

(see also complementary health, craniosacral therapy)

SUTHERLAND SOCIETY
15a Church Street, Bradford on Avon, BA15 1LN
0845 6030680
www.cranial.org.uk
For information regarding the cranial approach, including the treatment of babies & children

General Osteopathic Council
Osteopathy House, 176 Tower Bridge Road, London, SE1. 020 7357 6655

outdoor play equipment

(see also toy shops)

Goose Lane Activity Toys Centre
Heather Goose Lane, Little Hallingbury
01279 721467
Open easter-summer, Sats 10-2pm, Tue &Thu 5-8pm

Jungle Gym Activity Systems
Unit 46, Golds Nurseries Business Park, Jenkins Drive, Elsenham
01279 814686

outdoor play equipment (cont.)

Orchard End Activity Toy Centre
Orchard End, Bishops Stortford
01279 718263

Pepperstock Playframes
Pepsal End Farm, Pepperstock, Luton
01582 415900
www.pepperstockplayframesatc.co.uk

Wicken Activity Toys
Whittlebury Road, Wicken
01908 571233

TP Activity Toys
0800 068 1870
www.tptoys.com

outings

*(see also farms, indoor adventure playcentres,
museums, parks & open spaces, playgrounds,
theatres, theme parks, zoos)*

Always ring to check opening times and avoid
disappointment. If you are travelling outside
the area covered by this Baby Directory, don't
forget to arm yourself with the necessary Local
Baby Directory. We now cover

- **Bristol & Bath**
- **London**
- **Oxfordshire, Bucks & Berks**
- **South Wales**
- **Surrey & S. Middlesex**
- **Sussex & Hampshire**

Herts

Buntingford
Cromer Windmill
Ardeley. 01438 861662
Open 2nd and 4th w/ends in month & Bank
Hols in summer

Berkhamsted
Berkhamsted Castle
01604 730320
Open daily 10-4pm

Folly's Farm Sanctuary for Donkeys
off Nettleden Road, Potten End. 01442 871158
Sun pm May to Sept

Broxbourne
Adventuress River Cruises
Lee Valley Boat Centre, Old Nazeing Road
01992 466111
Public cruises during holidays

Hatfield
Hatfield House
01707 262823
House, gardens and park. Playground, model
soldiers exhibition. Picnics allowed, also
restaurant

Mill Green Mill
Mill Green, Hatfield. 01707 271362
Working mill, open Tue-Sun. Milling on Tue,
Wed, Sun. Museum next door

Rickmansworth
Batchworth Lock Centre
Church Street. 01923 778382
Canal boat trips on Batchworth Ferry Sundays
Easter to October, café, birthday parties.
Annual Canal Festival

Royston
Wimpole Hall
Arrington. 01223 207257
Combine with trip to Home Farm (*see farms*),
restaurant with kid menu and high chairs and
scribble sheets. National Trust

St Albans
Gardens of the Rose
Chiswell Green
01727 850461

Kingsbury Watermill
St Michaels Street
01727 853502

Stevenage
Knebworth House
01438 812661
Fort Knebworth adventure playground,
miniature railway. House not really suitable
for children. Café. Maze

Ware
Scott's Grotto
Scotts Road. 01920 464131
Underground passages and chambers - bring a
torch! Not suitable for pushchairs
Sats + Bank Holiday Mondays, 2-4.30pm,
April-September

Watford
Arcturus Boat Trips
Ironbridge Lock, Cassiobury Park, Watford
01438 714528
Cruise through Cassiobury Park, Sundays
Easter–October

Welwyn Garden City
Rollercity
Campus West, The Campus
01707 357117
Roller skating for all ages and abilities

Middx

Brentford
Syon Park - Aquatic Experience & London
Butterfly House
Aquatic Experience 020 8847 4730
London Butterfly House 020 8560 7272
Syon House & Park 020 8568 0883
House, gardens, garden centre, café, and
aquatic and butterfly attractions. Also Snakes
& Ladders indoor adventure playground

Heathrow Airport
Heathrow Airport Visitor Centre
off the Northern Perimeter Road, Heathrow
Airport. 020 8745 6655
Watch the planes!

Yeading
Willow Tree Narrow Boat Trips
Willow Tree Marina, West Quay Drive
020 8841 2100
Narrow boat trips on Grand Union Canal

Further afield
Berks

Bracknell
Look Out Discovery Park
Nine Mile Road, 01344 868 222
Environmental family park. Combine with
Coral Reef. M4, Jct 10, A322 signs for Bagshot
see swimming

Windsor
Legoland
Winkfield Road, Windsor. 0990 040 404
Jct 6 off M4, Jct 3 off M3. Train from Waterloo
+ shuttle bus

Windsor Castle
01753 868286

Bucks

Beaconsfield
Bekonscot Model Village
Warwick Road. 01494 672919
Open mid Feb-mid Nov. 1950's style model
village with miniature trains, also playground
and café

Chalfont St Giles
Chiltern Open Air Museum
Newlands Park, Gorelands Lane. 01494 871117
20 reconstructed local buildings. Nature trails
and farm animals. Café

Milton Keynes
Gulliver's Land
Livingstone Drive, Newlands
01908 609001
Over 30 rides and attractions, end Mar-Oct

www.
BABY
directory.com
Local up-dates

outings (cont.)

London

Changing the Guard
Buckingham Palace, The Mall.
Daily 11.30am from April to end of July.
Alternate days in winter

HMS Belfast
Morgan's Lane, off Tooley Street
020 7940 6300

Imax Cinema
Roundabout, Waterloo Station. 020 7902 1234
UK's biggest screen

London Aquarium
County Hall, Westminster Bridge Road
020 7967 8000

London Frog Tours
County Hall, Riverside Buildings,
Westminster Bridge Road. 020 7928 3132
Amphibious craft, river and road tour.
Summer only

The London Butterfly House
Syon Park, Brentford. 020 8560 0378
Tropical butterflies, toads, iguanas. Aquarium.
Can be combined with Snakes and Ladders
indoor adventure playground and the garden
centre

The London Eye
Jubilee Gardens. 0870 5000 600
Bit dull for tinies – and no getting off half-way!

London Planetarium
Marylebone Road. 020 7935 6861

Madame Tussaud's
Baker Street. 0870 400 3000
Too frightening for tinies. And the queue…
Tube to Baker Street

Royal Mews
Buckingham Palace. 020 7930 4832

Tower of London
Tower Hill. 020 7709 0765
Mon-Sat 9-6pm, winter 9.30-5pm. Sun 10-6pm,
winter 10-5pm. Tube to Tower Hill

Surrey

Chertsey
Thorpe Park
Staines Road
0870 444 44 66
White knuckle water rides

Chessington
Chessington World of Adventures
Leatherhead Road, Chessington
01372 729560
Theme park and zoo. Jct 9 off M25 or A3

East Molesey
Hampton Court Palace
020 8781 9500
Children's trail and maze. M25 Jct 10,
A307 or Jct 12, A308

parent & toddler groups

(see also mother & baby groups, playgroups)

These are mainly for parents or carers with children under three years, but some extend to under 5s. Usually run by parents, they are held in church halls, etc, and carers remain with the children. There is usually a small charge. Ring your local council *(see councils)* for venues near you, or check notice boards in clinics, hospitals and libraries

West Watford Network
01923 442158
Parents with pre-school children who voluntarily offer a range of activities for the und er 5's and mums/carers in the West Watford area. Expectant mums also welcome

parentcraft classes & advice

Parentalk
020 7450 9073

Parenting Education & Support Forum
020 7284 8370

The Parent Company
020 7935 9635

Harrow
Harrow Family Learning Network
020 8907 9356
Classes in all aspects of parenting

Watford
Handling Children's Behaviour Courses
Garston Clinic, 499 St Albans Road
01923 243568

parks & open spaces

(see also outings)

Herts

Barnet
Trent Country Park
Cockfoster Road
413 acres with visitor centre, café and children's animal corner

Moat Mount and Scratchwood Countryside Park
Barnet Way, Barnet Gate
Also has children's playground

Berkhamsted
Ashridge Estate
4000 acres of open space and woodland with picnic sites

Cheshunt
Cedars Park
Theobalds Lane
Pets Corner and water garden

Cheshunt Country Park
Park Lane
Open spaces and woodland

East Hertfordshire
Lee Valley Park
01992 702200 (information centre)
Includes farms, nature reserves, open spaces and waterways

Elstree
Aldenham County Park
Dagger Lane
Pooh Bears 100 Aker Wood, lake, children's and toddler's play area, farm area, kiosk, picnic tables. Recommended. Take three £1 coins for the car park

Visit us at
www.babydirectory.com

parks & open spaces (cont.)

Hatfield
Hatfield House
Hatfield. 01707 262823
Play area, picnic area, gift shops and
exhibitions, restaurant. Recommended

Hemel Hempstead
Gadebridge Park
River, flower gardens, playground and
paddling pool

Hertford
Hartham Common
Hartham Lane
Walks by the river

Rickmansworth
Aquadrome
Frogmore Lane
Two big lakes, canal walks, playground.
Annual canal festival

Royston
Priory Gardens
Children's play area

St Albans
Clarence Park
Also recreation area with sandpit and
playground

Verulamium Park
Lakes, picnic areas, playgrounds, paddling
pools, toilets

Herts & Middlesex Wildlife Trust
Grebe House, St Michaels Street
Wildlife displays and park

Stevenage
Benington Lordship Gardens
01438 869668
Open Wed & Sun. April to end of September.
Snowdrop openings Feb/Mar. Animal trail &
castle ruins. Teas in summer

Fairlands Valley Park
Six Hills Way
Children's boating lake, play area, paddling
pools

Whomerley & Monkswood
Broadhall Way
Ancient woodlands

Tring
Tring Park
via Akeman Street
300 acres, ideal for walking

Tring Reservoirs
Lower Ickneild Way, Marsworth
See the ducks and geese

Ware
Priory Park
The Priory, High Street
7 acres including playground, open air pool,
restaurant and coffee shop

Watford
Cassiobury Park
Cassiobury Park Avenue
190 acres including riverside and canal walks.
Good playground, paddling pools and
miniature railway. Recommended

Cheslyn Gardens
Nascot Wood Road
Watford's secret garden

Whippendell Woods
Grove Mill Lane
Ancient woodlands. Connects with Cassiobury
Park

Wheathamstead
No Man's Land Common
Large open space

Middx

Denham
Denham Country Park
Court Drive, off M40 (junct 1)
Visitor Centre for Colne Valley Park.
Children's coot trail

Northmoor Hills Woods
Tilehurst Lane, off North Orbital Road (A412)

Enfield
Capel Manor Gardens
Bullsmoor Lane. 01992 763849
Also farm corner with pigs, chickens and
horses. Recommended

Forty Hall Park
Forty Hill
Café and shop, house not suitable for small
children

Hillyfields Park
Clay Hill
Grassland and woodland. Nice walks

Harefield
**Bayhurst Wood County Park and Ruislip
Woods**
Brakespear Road North, Harefield
BBQ griddles for picnics

Harrow
Harrow Weald Common / Grimsdyke
Old Redding Road, off Common Road
Large open space

Hanwell
Bunny Park
Brent Lodge Park Animal Centre,
Cuckoo Lane
Café, play area, lots of animals including
rabbits, wallabees and donkeys.
Recommended

Hayes
Yeading Brooks Meadow
The Greenway

Hendon
Welsh Harp
Brent Reservoir
Playgrounds and picnic area

Isleworth
Osterley Park
01494 755566 infoline
National Trust property, large grounds,
tearoom, house not suitable for pushchairs or
backpacks. Recommended

Kingsbury
Fryent Country Park
Fryent Way. 020 8206 0492

Ruislip
Ruislip Lido and Park Woods
off Bury Street
Large woodlands with walks round the Lido
(see playgrounds). Grazing cows in summer

Southall
Glade Lane Countryside Park

Slough
Burnham Beeches
Hawthorn Lane, Farnham Common, Slough
Large ancient woodlands

West Drayton
Frays Island
Footpath from Thorney Mill Road

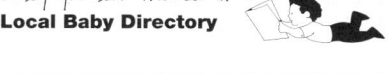

ACE ENTERTAINMENTS
01442 250039/07967 114170
Magic, balloon modelling & face painting for
all ages

Adam Ants
020 8959 1045

Adventures in Music
020 8958 2417
See advert under music

Please say you saw the ad in
The Local Baby Directory

party entertainers (cont.)

Amazing Spangles
020 8429 1146
The funny fairy

Applejack the Clown
01727 860445

Art Explosion
01923 681313

Be My Bear
020 8998 8483
Bring a bear to life

Busy Bee Children's Shows
01442 258339

Derilea, the man of magic
020 8904 5076

Dilly the Duck Magic Show
01582 486818

Dressed for Anything (dressing up parties)
01727 827076

Happy Times
020 8207 3737

Honky Tonks
01923 857386
See advert under music

Impeyan Productions
01992 446211
Animal Encounters and magic

Jane Mount Facepainting
01442 213271
Face painting & balloon modelling

Jenny Mayers
020 8908 0502

Jenty the Clown
020 8207 0437

Julian the Juggler
01442 213271

Visit us at
www.babydirectory.com

Kidazz
020 8866 8171
Activity parties

Kids Baking Parties
01923 778353

Liz Smelly Socks
020 8868 1988

Messy Play
020 8959 9045
2yrs+

Mini Makeovers
020 8398 6769/0107

Miss Makeover
01923 853833

Mr Chuckles
020 8428 4506

Musical Minis
01920 831177
See advert under music

MyNewt Enterprises
020 8805 0745
Cold blooded animal encounters (snakes etc)

Oscar & Orlando
01707 895973

Pippa Reid Children's Entertainer
020 8866 4232
Musical fun & stories

Popstarz
020 8428 1983

Sherbert the Clown
01442 259751
Lady clown

Simple Simon Says
020 8950 2571

Smartie Artie
01582 483977

Splat Children's Entertainer
01895 239195

Tricardo
01621 774477

Tricky Micky
01582 864885

Twizzle Parties
020 8392 6788

Uncle Smartie
01442 263418

The Wonder Bus
020 8968 3798
www.wonderbus.co.uk

party organisers

PARTIES-4-U
01462 732329
parties-4-u@which-net
www.parties-4-u.co.uk
Children's Parties, 1st Birthday, Christenings.
Tableware, Decorations, Balloons,
Entertainment, Cakes

P S Party Specialists
01462 892169

party equipment

(see also fancy dress, party entertainers)

ABDAB PARTY COMPANY
020 8441 7733
info@abdab.co.uk
www.abdab.co.uk
Party tableware, balloon décor, activities,
entertainment, fancy dress

I LOVE BALLOONS LTD
020 8904 0004
www.Iloveballoons.co.uk
Children's themed party balloons, party décor,
table centrepieces and party accessories

Bouncers (UK) Bouncy Castles
0800 0830577

Bouncy Fun Inflatables
01438 220177

Bouncy Tots
01442 872515

County Castles
01992 300630

Party Zone
01277 226999
www.partyzone.co.uk

Partyco
020 8995 1782
www.partyco.co.uk

Party Pieces
01635 201844

party shops

Eastcote
Sniggers Party Shop
103 Field End Road
020 8868 7323

Harrow
Giggles Party Shop
11 Headstone Drive, Wealdstone
020 8863 3691

Hayes
Giggles Party Shop
Bridge House, 119-123 Station Road
020 8848 7372

Hertford
Party World
20 St Andrew Street
01992 553618

Kenton
Funtasia
229 Kenton Road
020 8907 1333

Ruislip
Special Occasions
29-31 High Street
01895 633606

party shops (cont.)

Stanmore
Balloon & Party Shop
22 The Broadway
0800 6523023

Stevenage
A Special Occasion
28 Linkways
01438 369888

party venues

Try swimming pools, indoor adventure
playgrounds, farms, church halls, arts centres
and leisure centres

paternity testing

CELLMARK DIAGNOSTICS
PO Box 265, Abingdon, Oxfordshire
01235 528000
www.cellmark.co.uk
5-day DNA test. Phone customer services for
confidential advice

personal trainers

(see also exercise classes, health clubs with crèches)

All these specialise in ante and postnatal
fitness

Fiona Farrell
01923 441144

Julian Ivory
01438 821470

Nina Quattrone
020 8367 6784

Premier 1 to 1
020 8866 1734

photo albums

Creative Memories
01753 888902
Instruct in making personal family albums

photographers specialising in babies & children

Rickmansworth
VICTOR SHACK PHOTOGRAPHY
87 High Street, Rickmansworth
01923 772262
www.victorshackphotography.co.uk
Have a memory for a lifetime. Studio & home
portraits

St Albans
CAROLINE WILLIAMS
PHOTOGRAPHY
16 Sheppards Close
01727 757653
Baby / child portraits - friendly home studio -
time for outfit changes

Herts

Barnet
Derek Morley Photography
41 Clifford Road. 020 8441 6162

Bishops Stortford
David Cooper
24 Hockerill Street. 01279 755233

Elstree
Captured Moments
5 Woodside. 020 8207 1971

Hemel Hempstead
The Portrait Studio
50 St Mary's Road. 01442 254452

Hitchin
Derek George Photography
34 Bucklersbury. 01462 435093

Radlett
Brian Harris Family Portraits
Studio B, 1 Watford Road. 01923 856545

St Albans
Ian Lamond Photography
31 Stanley Avenue, Chiswell Green
01727 862972

Tring
Hyatt Studios
74 High Street. 01442 824747

Welwyn Garden City
Travelling Light
27 Dellcott Close. 01707 375992
Home portraits

Middx

Eastcote
Paul Rose Photography
186 Field End Road. 020 8866 1679

Harrow
George Wells Studios
325 Kenton Road. 020 8907 7741

Pinner
Frances Berger Photography
12 Murray Crescent. 020 8866 9040

Southall
Snowdon Photography
98 Ascot Gardens. 020 8578 9564

physiotherapists

Pinner Road Physiotherapy
97 Pinner Road, Harrow
020 8861 6001
www.physiolink.com
Specialist in pelvic floors

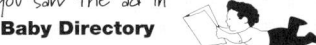

playcentres

Hayes
Lime Trees Playcentre
Thondike Avenue
020 8845 2514
Mon-Fri 12-7pm. Mother & toddler group in
afternoons, then after school club

Northolt
Islip Manor Playcentre
Eastcote Lane
020 8845 0231
Mon-Fri 12-3.30pm, drop in session with child

Southall
Dormers Wells Playcentre
Longridge Lane
020 8571 9756
Mother & toddler group 11–3pm, then after
school club for 5yrs+

playgrounds

(see also adventure playgrounds, indoor adventure playcentres, parks & open spaces, outings)

This is not a complete list of all the playgrounds in the area, but the largest or ones that have been particularly recommended

Herts

Barnet
Oak Hill Park
Parkside Gardens
Playground and lots of open space

Bishops Stortford
Castle Cardens & Sworders Field
Paddling pool in summer

Bushey
King George Recreation Ground
Perry Mead
Separate toddler and children's playgrounds. Sandpit and paddling pool

Hatfield
Welham Green Recreation Ground
Dellsome Lane, North Mymms

Hemel Hempstead
Gadebridge Park
Hemel Hempstead
Toddler play area as well as playground, paddling pool

Hertford
Bentley Road Playground

Castle Grounds
The Wash

Hartham Common
Good playground

Hitchin
Bancroft Recreation Ground
Nightingale Road

Hoddesdon
Barclay Park
Cock Lane

Letchworth
Howard Gardens
Norton Way South
Playground and paddling pool, toilets, recommended

London Colney
Mom's Playing Field
Whitehorse Lane
Helter skelter slide, climbing frame, toddler swings, tables

Rickmansworth
Aquadrome
Frogmore Lane
Nice walk past the lakes from the car park to the playground. Feed the swans on the way

St Albans
Greenwood Park
Tippendell Lane

St Stephens Ave
Large park, swings climbing frame with slide

Verulamium Park
Near Cathedral
Large play area, paddling pool, toilets

Ware
Priory Gardens
High Street

Watford
Cassiobury Park
Watford
Bark covered playground, paddling pools in summer, picnic tables, toilets

Welwyn Garden City
Stanborough Park
Stanborough Road
Toilets & café

Middx

Enfield
Albany Park
Good selection of equipment plus paddling pool and toilets

Aylands Open Space
Bullsmoor Lane
Paddling pool in summer, toilets

Bush Hill Park
Lincoln Road

Town Park
Cecil Road
Paddling pool in summer, café, toilets

Hayes
Barra Hall Park
Church Road

Harrow
West Harrow Recreation Ground
Butler Road / Wilson Gardens
Separate younger children's area with swings, climbing and slides

Headstone Manor Recreation Ground
Pinner View Way
Duck pond, big play area with toddler area

Northwood
Acre Way
Selection of big and small equipment

Pinner
Pinner Village Gardens
Whittington Way
Large open space and fenced in playground

Pinner Memorial Park
Chapel Lane
Duck pond, small playground, slide set into bank

Ruislip
Ruislip Lido
Play equipment on beach area including sand play. Older equipment nearby. Train rides at weekends. Café and pub

Further afield

Golders Hill, NW11
Golders Hill Park, West Hill Avenue
Flower gardens, duck and flamingo ponds. Small animal section. Large sandpit. Café

Holland Park, W8
Great for small children. Large sandpit and playground for under 5's (south of park). Japanese garden, peacocks, café

Queens Park, NW10
Excellent play equipment split for younger and older children. Big sandpit. Children's entertainment in summer. Small animal area. Café

playgroups

Contact the Pre-School Learning Alliance on 020 7833 0991 for up-to-date information on your local playgroup. For non PLA playgroups, contact the Under 8s section at your local council *(see councils)*

portraits

(see also photographers)

National Portraiture Association
020 7602 0892
www.natportrait.com

Kaidy Lewis
01707 376339

postnatal support & information

(see also breastfeeding, helplines: postnatal advice, mother & baby groups)

National Childbirth Trust
Alexandra House, Oldham Terrace,
London, W3. 0870 444 8707

pram & buggy repair

For details of major manufacturers ask at the shop where you bought the pram, or check our list of manufacturers and suppliers

London Nursery Supplies
Hardy Passage, Berners Road, London, N22
020 8889 3003

premature babies

Bliss: National Charity for the New Born
68 South Lambeth Road, London, SW8
0500 618140

www.premature-babies.co.uk

psychologists & psychotherapists

Child Psychotherapy Trust
Star House, 104-108 Grafton Road,
London NW5. 020 7284 1355

Association of Child Psychotherapists
020 8458 1609

Visit us at
www.babydirectory.com

pubs with playgrounds or playrooms

Aston
The Crown
56 Long Lane, Aston End. 01438 880060
Playground

Buntingford
The Railway Inn
1 London Road. 01763 271374
Bouncy castle and playground

Croxley Green
The Artichoke
The Green. 01923 772565
Outside play area

Elstree
The Battleaxes
Elstree Road. 020 8953 1049
Restaurant and outdoor play area

Hatfield
Airfield
Galleria Site, Lemsford Road. 01707 268990
Outdoor play equipment

Hertford
Cowper Arms
55 Cole Green Lane, Letty Green. 01707 330202
Outdoor play equipment

Hitchin
The Anchor
84 Cambridge Road. 01462 432091
Playarea in garden

Angels Reply
Bedford Road. 01462 450219
Indoor play area

The Millstream
97 Cambridge Road. 01462 434227
Playground outside, and separate children's area

Royal Oak
4 London Road, Chapelfoor, Langley,
Nr Hitchin. 01462 432653
Outdoor play equipment

St Albans
The Old Forge
Broadwater Crescent. 01438 351854
Charlie Chalks fun factory (indoor play)

South Oxhey
Brookdene Arms
Green Lane. 01923 224454
Charlie Chalks fun factory

Tring
Grand Junction Arms
Bulbourne. 01442 890677
Outdoor toddler play area and children's playground

Watton at Stone
The Bull
High Street. 01920 831032
Play area outdoors

Wheathampstead
Wicked Lady
14 Normansland Common. 01582 832128
Outdoor play equipment

Middx

Edgware
Jolly Badger Big Steak Pub
128 Hale Lane. 020 8959 6403
Outdoor play area

Enfield
Whitewebbs House
Whitewebbs Lane, Clay Hill. 020 8363 0542
Outdoor play area

Greenford
Myllet Arms Hotel
Western Avenue. 020 8997 4624
Wacky Warehouse (indoor play)

The Railway
390 Oldfield Lane. 020 8578 1193
Outdoor play area

Harefield
Horse and Barge
Moorhall Road. 01895 834080
Outdoor play area, bouncy castle in summer

The Case is Altered
Old Redding, Harrow Weald. 020 8954 1002
Outdoor play area in large garden

Horsenden Hill
The Ballot Box
Horsenden Lane North. 020 8902 2825
Wacky Warehouse (indoor play)

Ruislip
Breakspear Arms
Breakspear Road South. 01895 632239
Bouncy castle in summer

The Six Bells
Ducks Hill Road. 01895 639466
Garden with play equipment

The Waters Edge
Reservoir Road, Ruislip Lido. 01895 625241
Charlie Chalks fun factory (indoor play)

Wembley
The Green Man
Dagmar Avenue. 020 8903 1441
Outdoor play area

pushchairs: all-terrain

Pegasus Pushchairs Ltd
Westbridge, Tavistock, Devon
01462 450432

Practical Pushchairs Ltd
Pump Cottage, Wheathold, Wolverton,
Hampshire. 0118 981 7372

PW Trading Ltd
PO Box 506, St Albans, Herts AL4 0LT
01727 811221

Please say you saw the ad in
The Local Baby Directory

Give us your opinions on-line

rattles

Plate, Rattle and Bowl
38 Burwood Road, Northampton
01604 406320
www.babies-rattles.co.uk
We specialise in the craft of hand-made
wooden babies' rattles

reflexologists

(see also complementary health)

The British School of Reflexology
92 Sheering Road, Old Harlow
01279 429060
www.footreflexology.com

British Reflexology Association
Monks Orchard, Whitbourne, Worcs
01886 821207
www.britreflex.co.uk

registration of births

(see also naming ceremonies)

You have six weeks to decide on "its" name
before you must register your baby with your
local Registry Office

restaurants: child-friendly

(see also pubs with playgrounds or playrooms)

These restaurants usually have high chairs and
changing facilities. Some also offer crayons,
toys or entertainers

restaurant chains

Beefeater
www.beefeater.co.uk for local restaurants
Baby food, high chairs, children's meals

Brewer's Fayre
www.brewersfayre.co.uk for local restaurants
Baby food, high chairs, children's meals

Harvester
Baby food, high chairs, children's meals

John Lewis, The Place to Eat
Baby food, high chairs, children's lunch boxes

Supermarket cafés
Usually offer baby food, children's meals
(often with a toy), high chairs, baby change

other restaurants
Herts

Berkhamsted
Café Rouge
High Street. 01442 878141

Bishops Stortford
Caffe Uno
2-4 North Street. 01279 755725

Bushey
Quincy's
Elton Way. 01923 229137

The Windmill
107 High Road, Bushey Heath. 020 8950 1540

Chorleywood
The Peppermill
7 New Parade. 01923 284421
Reader recommended

Hertford
Café Rouge
3 Parliament Square. 01992 535363

Caffé Uno
17 Fore Street. 01992 504674

Hitchin
Pizza Express
19 Market Place. 01462 450596

Pizza Piazza
Bancroft. 01462 421101

The Tea & Coffee House
Market Place. 01462 433631

Kings Langley
Oscars Pizza Company
21 High Street. 01923 263800

Letchworth
Daisies Coffee Shop
Leys Avenue. 01462 676382

Rickmansworth
Long Island Exchange Bar Diner
2 Victoria Close (opp Met Station)
01923 779466

St Albans
Bella Pasta
21-23 Chequers Street. 01727 844264

Clauds Creperie
15 Holywell Hill. 01727 846424

Gatsby's Tearooms
17 High Street. 01727 811890

Waterend Barn
St Peters Street. 01727 848643

Zizzi
by the Clock Tower. 01727 883020

Watford
Café Mezza Lebanese Grill
144 High Street. 01923 211500

Pizza Express
Lower High Street. 01923 213991

Middx

Enfield
Charlie's Pizza
13-14 Colman Parade, Southbury Road
020 8367 8549

Chiquito Restaurant & Bar
492 Great Cambridge Road. 020 8367 9991

Enzo's Ristorante
88 Chaseside. 020 8363 6974

Nelito's Ristorante
61-63 Windmill Hill. 020 8366 0595

Harrow
Blubeckers Restaurant
Brooks Hill, Harrow Weald. 020 8954 4949

Golden Palace
148 Station Road. 020 8424 8899
Chinese. Reader recommended

Northwood
ASK Pizza and Pasta
35a Green Lane. 01923 842182

Pinner
ASK Pizza & Pasta Restaurant
Uxbridge Road, Hatch End. 020 8421 6789

Café Rouge
13 High Street. 020 8429 4424

Caffe Uno
15-17 High Street. 020 8429 3239

Pizza Siena
461 Uxbridge Road, Hatch End
020 8420 2100

Ruislip
Blubeckers Eating House
The Old Duck House, 2a/2b High Street
01895 622766

Uxbridge
ASK Pizza & Pasta
139 High Street. 01895 272799

Restaurant, Debenhams
The Chimes Shopping Centre
01895 814200
Babyfood, children's meals, high chairs,
breastfeeding room.
Reader recommended

re-training

Been out of the office for a year or two? Worried that you are hopelessly out of date? Need a refresher course, or just a bit of mental stimulation after all that posseting and nappy talk? Check out Adult Education classes (some offer creches), the Open University, your Local Authority careers advice. Look in local papers, the library, buy a copy of Floodlight (available at newsagents) for all London course listings

riding

Bishops Stortford
Hallingbury Hall Equestrian Centre
Little Hallingbury. 01279 730348
4yrs+

Forest Stables Riding Centre
Leapers Lane, Great Hallingbury. 01279 758051
5yrs+

Bushey
The Lincolnsfield Riding Centre
Bushey Hall Drive. 01923 240127
3yrs+

Harpenden
Greenacres Riding School
Lower Luton Road. 01582 760612
3yrs+

Hemel Hempstead
Gaddesdon Place Stables
Gaddesden Place. 01442 252446
6yrs+

Visit us at
www.babydirectory.com

Hitchin
Ickleford Equestrian Centre
Lower Green Farm, Ickleford. 01462 459081

Kings Langley
Kings Langley Riding School
Whippendell Spinney, Chipperfield Road
01923 270719
3yrs+

Rickmansworth
Coltspring Riding School
Sarratt Road, Chandlers Cross. 01923 774964

Ware
Contessa Riding Centre
Willow Tree Farm, Colliers End. 01920 821792
From 3yrs with parents help

Watford
Watford Equestrian Centre
37 Bucks Avenue. 01923 212670
Tots sessions 2-5yrs in holidays, junior rides from 4yrs

Middx

Harrow Weald
Suzanne's Riding School
Brookshill Farm, Brookshill Drive
020 8954 3618
5yrs+

Hillingdon
Goulds Green Riding School
Goulds Green. 01895 446256
4yrs+

rocking horses

(see also nursery furniture)

Furzedown Rocking Horses
Standalone Farm, Wilbury Way, Letchworth
01462 487517

Robert Mullis
01793 813583

Stevenson Brothers
0808 108 6120

safety advice

Child Accident Prevention Trust (CAPT)
18-20 Farringdon Lane, London, EC1
020 7608 3828

Nannycam
24 Parr Road, London, E6. 020 8471 8616
Hidden camera rental

school consultants

GABBITAS EDUCATIONAL CONSULTANTS
Carrington House,
126-130 Regent Street, London, W1
020 7734 0161
admin@gabbitas.co.uk
www.gabbitas.com

ISCis London & South East
020 7798 1560
www.iscis.uk.net/southeast

schools: pre-prep

(see also helplines: education, nurseries: day)

For a list of state schools in your area, contact your local council *(see councils)*. ISCis or Gabbitas can also supply information on private schools in your area.

For a list of state schools in your area, contact your local council *(see councils)*

Barnet
Lyonsdown School and Nursery
3 Richmond Road. 020 8449 0225
Boys 3-7yrs, girls 3-11yrs

Norfolk Lodge Nursery Prep School
Golders Hill Road. 020 8447 1565
Co-ed 2-11yrs

Please say you saw the ad in
The Local Baby Directory

schools: pre-prep (cont.)

St Martha's Junior
22 Wood Street. 020 8449 4346
Girls 4-11yrs

Berkhamsted
Berkhamsted Collegiate School
Overton, 131 High Street. 01442 358002
Co-ed 3-18yrs

Egerton-Rothesay School
Durrants Lane. 01442 865275
Co-ed 2-18yrs

Haresfoot School
Chesham Road. 01442 872742

Bishop's Stortford
Bishops Stortford Junior College
Maze Green Road. 01279 838607
Co-ed 4-13yrs

Bushey
St Hilda's School
High Street. 020 88950 1751
Girls 3-11yrs

St Margarets School
Bushey. 020 8950 1548
Girls 4-18yrs

Elstree
Haberdashers' Aske's School for Girls
Aldenham Road. 020 8266 2303
Girls 4-18yrs

Harpenden
Aldwickbury School
Whearhampstead Road. 01582 713022
Boys 4-13yrs, girls 4-6yrs

Harpenden Prep School
53 Luton Road. 01582 712361
Co-ed 2-11yrs

St Hilda's School
28 Douglas Road. 01582 712307
Girls 2-11yrs

Hemel Hempstead
Abbot's Hill
Bunkers Lane. 01442 240333
Boys 3-7yrs, girls 3-16yrs

Westbrook Hay
London Road. 01442 256143
Co-ed 2-13yrs

Hertford
Duncombe School
4 Warren Park Road, Bengeo. 01992 414100
Co-ed 2-11yrs

Hitchin
Kingshott School
St Ippolyts. 01462 432009
Co-ed 4-13yrs

Kings Langley
Rudolf Steiner School
Langley Hill
01923 262505
Co-ed 3^1/$_2$-19yrs

Letchworth
St Christopher School
01462 679301
Co-ed 2-19yrs

St Francis' College
Broadway. 01462 670511
Girls 3-18yrs

Milton Keynes
Milton Keynes Prep School
Tattenhoe Lane. 01908 642111
Boys 2^1/$_2$-11yrs

Potters Bar
Lochinver House School
Heath Road, Little Heath. 01707 653064
Boys 4-13yrs

St John's School
The Ridgeway. 01707 657294
Co-ed 5-11yrs

Stormont School
The Causeway. 01707 654037
Girls, 4-11yrs

Radlett
Manor Lodge School
Rectory Lane, Ridge Hill. 01707 642424
Co-ed 4-11yrs

Rickmansworth
THE ROYAL MASONIC SCHOOL FOR GIRLS
PO Box 356, Rickmansworth Park
01923 773168
enquiries@royalmasonic.herts.sch.uk
www.royalmasonic.herts.sch.uk
RMS provides excellent opportunities for all-round development

Northwood Preparatory School
Moor Farm, Sandy Lodge Road. 01923 825648
Boys 4-13yrs

Rickmansworth PNEU School
88 The Drive. 01923 772101
Girls 3-11yrs

York House School
Redheath, Croxley Green. 01923 772395
Boys 2-13yrs, girls 2-5yrs

St Albans
Beechwood Park
Markyate. 01582 840333
Co-ed 4-13yrs

Homewood Independent School
Hazel Road, Park Street. 01727 873542
Co-ed 3-8yrs

St Albans High School for Girls
Townsend Avenue. 01727 853800
Girls 4-18yrs

Tring
St Francis de Sales Independent Day School
Aylesbury Road. 01442 822315
Co-ed 2-11yrs

Ware
St Edmund's College
Old Hall Green. 01920 821504
Co-ed 3-18yrs. Catholic

Watford
Edge Grove
Aldenham. 01923 855724
Boys 2-13yrs, girls 2-7yrs

St Andrews Montessori School
High Elms Lane, Garston Manor
01923 663875
Co-ed 2-11yrs
See advert under nurseries

Stanborough School
Stanborough Park, Garston. 01923 673268
Co-ed 3-18yrs

Watton at Stone
Heath Mount School
Woodhall Park. 01920 830230
Co-ed 3-13yrs

Welwyn
Sherrardswood School
Lockleys. 01438 714282
Co-ed 2-19yrs

Middx

Brentford
Buttercups
The Garden House, Syon Park, London Road
020 8568 4355
4-7yrs

Edgware
Holland House School
1 Broadhurst Avenue. 020 8958 6979
Co-ed 4-11yrs

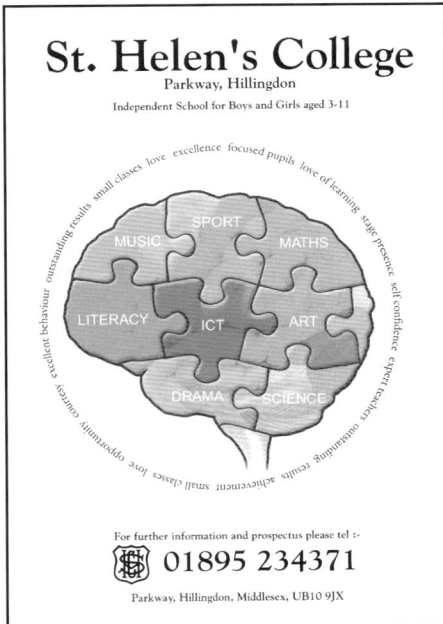

St. Helen's College

Parkway, Hillingdon

Independent School for Boys and Girls aged 3-11

For further information and prospectus please tel :-

01895 234371

Parkway, Hillingdon, Middlesex, UB10 9JX

schools: pre-prep (cont.)

North London Collegiate School
Canons. 020 8952 0912
Girls 4-18yrs

Harrow
Alpha Prep School
21 Hindes Road. 020 8427 1471
Co-ed 4-13yrs

Orley Farm School
South Hill Avenue. 020 8422 1525
Co-ed 4-13yrs

Quainton Hall School
Hindes Road. 020 8427 1304
Boys 4-13yrs

Hillingdon
ST HELEN'S COLLEGE
Parkway
01895 234371
Boys & girls age 3-11yrs

American Community School
Hillingdon Court, 108 Vine Lane. 01895 259771
Co-ed 3-18yrs

Northwood
The Hall Pre-Prep School
Rickmansworth Road. 01923 822807
Co-ed 4-11yrs

Northwood College
Maxwell Road. 01923 825446
Girls 3-18yrs

Northwood Preparatory Boys School (Terrys)
Moor Farm, Sandy Lodge Road
01923 825648
Boys 4-13yrs

St Helen's School
Eastbury Road. 01923 828511
Girls 4-18yrs

St John's School
Potter Street Hill. 020 8866 0067
Boys 4-13yrs

St Martin's School
40 Moor Park Road. 01923 825740
Boys 3-13yrs

Pinner
Buckingham College Prep School
458 Rayners Lane, Rayners Lane
020 8866 2737
Boys 3-11yrs

Heathfield School
Beaulieu Drive. 020 8868 2346
Girls 3-18yrs

Innellan House School
44 Love Lane. 020 8866 1855
Co-ed 3-8yrs

Reddiford School
38 Cecil Park. 020 8866 0660
Co-ed 3-11yrs

Stanmore
Peterborough & St Margarets School
Tanglewood, Common Road. 020 8950 3600
Girls 4-16yrs

Wembley
Buxlow Preparatory School
5/6 Castleton Gardens, East Lane
020 8904 3615
Co-ed 4-11yrs

St Christopher's School
71 Wembley Park Drive. 020 8902 5069
Co-ed 4-11yrs

sex choice

Materna S.A.
PO Box 21947, London ,SW3 2ZU
020 7225 3234

shoes

(see also mail order)

BOBUX
07002 466466
direct@goo-goo.com
www.goo-goo.com
Original soft leather shoes for under twos with stayonability!

SHOO SHOOS
Hippychick Ltd, Barford Gables,
Spaxton, Somerset. 01278 671461
sales@hippychickltd.co.uk
www.hippychickltd.co.uk
Imaginative and refreshingly different, soft leather baby shoes (0-24 months)

SOLE MANIA
07002 466466
www.goo-goo.com
direct@goo-goo.com
Durable washable leather slippers for unstoppable nippers aged 2ish to 90ish!

Pitter Patter
Tring. 01442 825753
Soft leather bootees

Starchild Shoes
109 Paget Street, Loughborough, Leics
01509 550714
www.star-child.co.uk

Sarah Page Sculpture
020 7207 0884
Your child's first shoe plated in copper or silver

shoe shops

Barnet
Instep
267 East Barnet Road
020 8440 9860

Berkhamsted
Colton
240 High Street
01442 863562

Bishops Stortford
Solely for Children
8-9 Florence Walk
01279 501777

Eastcote
Pidgeons
243 Field End Road
020 8868 5386

Harpenden
Galloways
2 Bowers Parade, High Street
01582 712993

Hillingdon
Beekay Shoes
2 Crescent Parade
01895 234458

Hoddesdon
Strides of Hoddesdon
57 High Street
01992 442120

Letchworth
Burrs Shoes
7-9 Leys Avenue
01462 686080

Northwood
Bowleys Shoes
7 Clive Parade, Green Lane
01923 825231

Please say you saw the ad in
The Local Baby Directory

shoe shops (cont.)

Radlett
Instep
275 Watling Street
01923 855226

Royston
Burrs
43 High Street
01763 243215

St Albans
Footsteps
15 High Street
01727 837393

Stanmore
Bowleys Shoes
34 Church Road
020 8954 6381

Brians Children's Shoes
68 The Broadway
020 8954 3712

Ware
Burrs Shoes
15 High Street
01920 464179

Watford
Gordon Scott Ltd
Harlequin Centre
01923 229163

shopping crèches

Shop in peace!

Brent Cross
Nipperboat Playcentre
Brent Cross Shopping Centre
020 8202 3667
2-8yrs

Brent Park
Ikea
020 8208 5600
Ball pond & activities

St Albans
Safeway
244 Hatfield Road
01727 830097
2-8yrs

Uxbridge
Chimes Chums
303 The Chimes Shopping Centre, High Street
01895 251155
2-7yrs, Mon-Sun

Watford
Asda
Asda Superstore
01923 250380
2-8yrs

Harlequin Shoppers Crèche
201 The Harlequin
01923 250292
Shoppers creche, kiddykarts for hire

Tesco Kid's Club
Tesco Superstore, 239 -241 Lower High Street
01923 486477
Also available for birthday parties

Watford Women's Centre Crèche
Lower Mall, 20 Charter Place
01923 240964
From 2yrs 9mths-6yrs

single parents

(see also helplines)

Gingerbread
020 7488 9300

Kids No Object
Lymington, Farwell Avenue, Eastergate,
Chichester, West Sussex
01243 543685
Introduction agency for single parents

Single Parent Travel Club
0870 241 6210

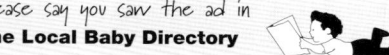

ski companies specialising in children

Chilly Powder
020 7289 6958

Mark Warner
0870 8480 482

Meriski
01451 843100

Simply Ski
020 8541 2207

Ski Beat
01243 780405

Ski Company
01451 843123

Ski Famille
01223 363777

Ski Olympic
01709 579999

Ski Scott Dunn
020 8767 0202

Ski Solutions
020 7471 7733

Snowbizz Vacances
01778 341455

ski slopes: artificial

Bassingbourn Ski Centre
Royston. 01763 848114

Gosling Ski Centre
Gosling Sports Park, Stanborugh Road,
Welwyn Garden City. 01707 384384

Hemel Ski Centre
St Albans Hill. 01442 241321

Snozone
Milton Keynes. 01908 230260
Real snow!

Wycombe Summit
Abbey Barn Lane, High Wycombe
01494 474711
Lessons from 3yrs

skincare

E45 JUNIOR
Available from all leading supermarkets and pharmacies
www.e45.com
Dermatologist and paediatrician approved.
Developed for children with dry, sensitive skin or eczema

sleep

MILLPOND
020 8941 6370
www.mill-pond.co.uk
Specialist in children's sleep problems

Good Sleep Guide for You and Your Baby
PO Box 5868, Forres, IV36 1WH
07020 922750

sleeping bags

(see also linens)

BONNE NUIT
020 8871 1472
sales@bonne-nuit.co.uk
www.bonne-nuit.co.uk
Beautiful French baby sleeping bags available
in 3 sizes (0-4yrs). (Winter & summer
collection). Call for brochure or stockist, or
order online

Clair de Lune
Shentonfield Road, Wythenshawe, Manchester
0161 491 9800

Grobag
01548 854444
www.grobag.com

Little Star
01737 371221

slimming

Numbers are central information lines.
Call for details of your local class

Rosemary Conley Diet and Fitness Clubs
01509 620222

Slimming World
01773 521111

Weight Watchers
08457 123000

spanish

Escuela Madrid
Hemel Hempstead
01442 247237

story tellers

Story Tellers Association
PO Box 2344, Reading
0118 935 1381

sun protection

SPOSH
07002 466 466
direct@goo-goo.com
www.goo-goo.com
Original UPF50+ swimwear to beat the sun but
still have fun!

swimming classes

(see also swimming pools)

Most local swimming pools run classes for
babies and young children

Herts

LITTLE FISHES
Hatfield
01707 276734
A calm and gentle introduction to water for
infants from 4 months

Dolphin Swim School
01305 823592
Digswell

In the Swim
Cheshunt School Swimming pool
07932 595599

Making Waves with Cyndy
020 8420 2013
Bushey. From 2$^{1}/_{2}$yrs

Starting Blocks Swimming School
Hemel Hempstead
01442 241030

Visit us at
www.babydirectory.com

Tony Woodhams Swimming Club
Monkswalk Pool, Welwyn Garden City
01707 330578
From 4-11yrs

Middx

Aquastyle
020 8931 1811
Northwood & Bushey

Carolann's Aqua Tots
01923 236473
Northwood

Champions Swimming
01895 622382
Northwood. From toddlers

Flippers Swimming Club
020 8427 5255
Northwood

Goldfish Classes
Yiewsley Pool, Otterfield Road
01895 442444

Poolside Manor
020 8349 1945
Finchley

swimming pools: indoor

(see also health clubs with crèches, leisure centres)

Herts

Barnet
Church Farm Swimming Pool
Church Hill Road
020 8368 7070
Lessons, children's parties, parent and toddler sessions

Berkhamsted
Berkhamsted Sports Centre
Lagley Meadow, Douglas Gardens
01442 228123
Also children's pool

Bishops Stortford
Grange Paddocks Pool & Gym
Rye Street. 01279 652332
Also children's pool

Borehamwood
The Venue
Elstree Way. 020 8386 9886
Also teaching pool. Crèche

Broxbourne
Lee Valley Leisure Pool
Old Nazeing Road. 01992 467899
Wave machine, activity play zone, café, aqua tots session, baby pool

Buntingford
Ward Freman Pool
Bowling Green Lane. 01763 272566

swimming pools (cont.)

Cheshunt
Grundy Park Pool
Windmill Lane. 01992 623345
Crèche 9.30am-12.30pm Mon-Fri

Harpenden
Harpenden Sports Centre
Rothamsted Park, Leyton Road. 01582 460683
Also learner pool

Hatfield
Hatfield Swim Centre
Lemsford road. 01707 264487
Children's and learner pool. Crèche Mon-Fri
9am-5pm

Hemel Hempstead
Aqua Splash
Leisure world, Jarman Park. 01442 292203
Beach area, baby pool

Hertford
Hartham Pool
Hartham Common. 01992 584000
Also learner pool

Hitchin
Hitchin Swimming Centre
Fishponds Road. 01462 441646
Also children's pool

Potters Bar
Furzefield Centre
Mutton Lane. 01707 850500
Also teaching pool
See advert under leisure centres

Rickmansworth
William Penn Leisure Centre
Shepherds Lane, Mill End. 01923 771050
Creche 3mths-3yrs

Sawbridgeworth
Leventhorpe Swimming Pool
Cambridge Road. 01279 722490

South Oxhey
Sir James Altham Pool
Little Oxhey Lane. 020 8421 0211

Stevenage
Stevenage Swimming Centre
St Georges Way. 01438 218770
Also children's pool

Ware
Fanshawe Swimming Pool
Park Road, Fanshaw. 01920 466967

Watford
The Everett Centre
Leggatts Way. 01923 441444
Crèche Tue am

Watford Central Baths
Hempstead Road. 01923 221409
Ducklings crèche for 0-5yrs; Mon, Wed-Fri

Middx

Brentford
Fountain Leisure Centre
658 Chiswick High Road. 020 8944 9596
Leisure pool with waves, beach, fountains etc

Ealing
Gurnell Pool
Ruislip Road East. 020 8998 3241
Also learner pool

Enfield
Albany Swimming Pool
505 Hertford Road. 020 804 4222

Hayes
Hayes Pool
Central Lane, Central Avenue. 020 8573 2785

Hendon
Barnet Copthall Centre
Great North Way. 020 8457 9900
Baby sessions, swimming lessons from $3^1/2$yrs

Heston
Heston Pool
New Heston Road. 020 8570 4396
Also teaching pool

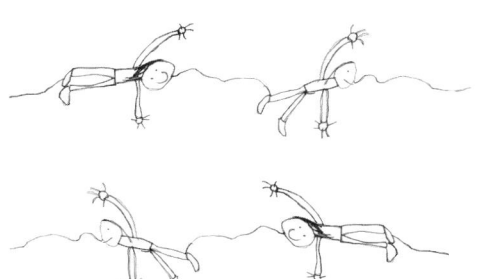

Northolt
Swimarama
Eastcote Lane. 020 8422 1176
Also small pool

Ruislip
Highgrove Swimming Pool
Eastcote Road. 01895 630753
Also learner pool

Southall
Dormers Wells Leisure Centre
Dormers Wells Lane. 020 8571 7207

Stanmore
Aspire
Royal National Orthopaedic Hospital,
Wood Lane. 020 8954 5759
Some public swim sessions

Wembley
Vale Farm Sports Centre
Watford Road. 020 8908 6545
Crèche 1-5yrs

Yiewsley
Yiewsley Pool
Otterfield Road. 01895 442444
Also children's pool

Further afield

Coral Reef
Nine Mile Ride, Bracknell, Berkshire
01344 862525
Superb fun pools with chutes, flumes, galleons,
currents

swimming pools: outdoor

Usually only open during the summer months
(May-Sept)

Compton Leisure Centre (Northolt)
Bengarth Road, Northolt
020 8841 0953

Hitchin Outdoor Pool
Fishponds Road
01462 441646
50m pool

Hoddesdon Open Air Swimming Pool
High Street
01992 461592

Letchworth Outdoor Pool
Icknield Way
01462 684673
50m pool + paddling pool

Priory Lido (Ware)
High Street
01920 460316

Royston Outdoor Pool
Newmarket Road
01763 245577
23m pool + paddling pool

tennis

Also check out your local leisure centre

Hillingdon
Hillingdon Academy of Tennis
01895 813746

Hoddesdon & Royston
Tactics Tennis School
01763 273646

St Albans
Batchwood Tennis & Golf Centre
Batchwood Drive
01727 844250

TENS machines

Pain relief without drugs

Babycare TENS
108 George Lane, London, E18. 020 8532 9595

Natures Gate
PO Box 371, Basingstoke, Hants
01256 346060

ObTens
2 Rosling Road, Horfield, Bristol
0117 951 4110

TensCare
020 8547 1999

Trust Tens
265 Park Road, Kingston, Surrey
020 8546 1616

theatres

(see also arts centres, drama)

Many theatres stage shows for children,
especially in school holidays and pantomimes
at Christmas

Bishops Stortford
Rhodes Centre
South Road. 01279 651746

Hemel Hempstead
Dacorum Pavilion
Marlowes. 01442 228700

Old Town Hall
High Street. 01442 228091

Hertford
Castle Hall
The Wash. 01992 589026

Hitchin
Market Theatre
6a Sun Street. 01462 433553

Queen Mother Theatre
Woodside, Walsworth Road. 01462 455166

Rickmansworth
Watersmeet Theatre
High Street. 01923 771542

St Albans
Alban Arena
Civic Centre. 01727 844488
Holiday shows and pantomime

Maltings Arts Theatre
Level 2, Maltings Shopping Centre
01727 844222

Stevenage
Gordon Craig Theatre
Lytton Way. 01438 766877

Tring
The Court Theatre
Station Road, Pendley. 01442 824673/4

Watford
Palace Theatre
Clarendon Road. 01923 225671 (booking)

Middx

Brentford
Watermans Arts Centre
40 High Street. 020 8847 5651 or 020 8568 1176
box office
Pandemonium (music), Weds am, under 2yrs
and 2-4yrs. Theatre club 5-8yrs

Ealing
Questors Theatre
Mattock Lane. 020 8567 5184
Drama for 5yrs+

Hayes
The Beck Theatre
Grange Road. 020 8561 8371

Ickenham
Compass Theatre & Arts Centre
Glebe Avenue. 01895 673200
Also summer 'fun factory' for children

London

Little Angel Theatre
14 Dagmar Passage, off Cross Street, N1
020 7226 1787

Puppet Theatre Barge
when moored on Regents Canal
020 7249 6876

Unicorn Theatre
St Mark's Studios, Chillingworth Road, N7
020 7700 0702

theme parks

(see also outings)

Alton Towers
Staffordshire. 0870 520 4060

Chessington World of Adventure
Surrey. 01372 727227

Disneyland
Marne-la-Vallee Cedex 4, France
0870 50 30 303

Efteling
Europalaan 1, Kaasheuvel, Netherlands
00-31-41 62288 111
Dutch theme park

Legoland
Berkshire. 01753 626100

Thorpe Park
Surrey. 01932 562633

toy libraries

Berkhamsted
Berkhamsted Toy Library
Gable Hall, Prince Edward Street
01442 894876
Alternate Thu, 9.30-11.30am

Borehamwood
Borehamwood Toy Library
Family Support Centre, Elstree Way
020 8953 1233
Mon 1-4pm, Fri 1-3.30pm

Harpenden
Harpenden Toy Library
Batford Nursery School, Holcroft Road
Wed, 9.30-11am, termtime

Hemel Hempstead
Grovehill Toy Library
Grovehill Youth Club, Stevenage Rise
01442 248194
Alternate Wed

Hertford
Hertford Toy Library
Sele School Youth Wing, Welwyn Road
01992 584227
Mon 9.30-11am

Letchworth
Noel Toy Library
1 Norton Way North
Fri 1-2.30pm termtime

Rickmansworth
WRVS Rickmansworth Toy Library
Bury Meadows, Bury Lane
01923 772096
9.30-11.30am, 2nd and 4th Weds each month
incl school hols

South Oxhey
Playbox
Otley Family Centre, Otley Way
020 8428 5233
Fri 10-12pm Wed 10-11am

St Albans
St Albans Toy Library
St Julian's Church Hall, 3 Abbotts Avenue
01727 843277
Tues10-12pm, term time

Stevenage
Stevenage Toy Library
Stevenage Arts & Leisure Centre
01438 242247
Tues & Fri 9.45-12.15pm term time

Tring
Tring Toy Library
Corpus Christi Church Hall, Langdon Street
01442 824462
Alternate Mon, 10-11.30am

toy libraries (cont.)

Ware
Ware Toy Library
Wodson Park
01920 870273
Mon 9.30-11am, term times, under 5's

Watford
Rainbow Toy Library
The Lemarie Centre, 524 St Albans Road
01923 220816
For children with special needs

Welwyn Garden City
Rainbow Toy Library
Cole Green Lane
01707 331686
Mon 10am-1pm, Fri 10am-1pm

Middx

Enfield
Moorfields Family Centre
2 Moorfield Road
020 8805 6313
Mon-Fri, 9.30-11am

Greenford
Windmill Toy Library
135 Windmill Lane
Tue 2.30-4.30pm, Wed 9.30-11.30am

Hayes
Toy Library
Immaculate Heart of Mary Church,
Botwell Lane
Alternate Tue

Northwood
Emmanuel Toy Library
Church Hall Complex, High Street
01923 821598
Thu am,term time,10-12.15pm

Southall
Disraeli Nursery Centre
111 Hamborough Road
020 8813 8078
12-3pm, Mon-Fri

Uxbridge
Uxbridge Community Toy Library
Uxbridge Resource Centre, 57 Park Road
01895 232539
Tues 2-4pm

West Drayton
Toys on Top
Bell Farm Christian Centre, South Road
Mon 1.30-4.30pm, Tues 4-7pm, Fri 11.30-2.30pm

toy shops

(see also mail order: toys)

Early Learning Centre and Mothercare have branches on many high streets

Herts

St Albans
LITTLE WONDERS
2 The Maltings
01727 863800
www.littlewonders.co.uk
In a world full of plastic it's nice to feel the quality of wood

Barnet
Harvey Johns
134 High Street
020 8449 0966

Berkhamsted
Hamlins Toy Shop
231 High Street
01442 864642

Borehamwood
Kindercare
130 Shenley Road
020 8953 7701

Harpenden
Felicitations
17 High Street
01582 767811

Lorna's Toys
4a Piggottshill Lane
01582 769204

Hatfield
Kids Play Factory
The Galleria, Comet Way
01707 258720

Letchworth
Harvey Johns
23 Eastcheap
01462 677119

Royston
The Toy Shop
25 High Street
01763 243270

Riders Toys
16-18 Chequer Street
01727 854638

Stevenage
The Entertainer
Unit 5, The Forum
01438 362521

Toys R Us
Roaring Meg Retail Park, London Road
01438 740174

Watford
Bear Factory
43 The Harlequin
01923 245304

Harvey Johns
39 Charter Place
01923 248334

Welwyn Garden City
Toys Toys Toys
47 Howard Centre, Howardsgate
01707 391319

Middx

Enfield
Jennings Toys
244 Hertford Road
020 8804 1804

Toys & Tales
37 Church Street
020 8363 9319

Toys R Us
7 Enfield Retail Park, Great Cambridge Road
020 8364 6600

Harrow
Grahams Toys
178-180 Alexandra Avenue, South Harrow
020 8422 2610
www.londontoycompany.co.uk

Ruislip
John Sanders Ltd
77-79 High Street
01895 634848

Southall
Toys 'R' Us
Hayes Road
020 8561 4681

Uxbridge
The Entertainer
The Pavilions Shopping Centre
01895 271200

trains

(see also museums, outings)

Harlington Locomotive Society
High Street, Harlington
Occasional train rides on a Sunday

Ickenham & District Miniature Railway Society
Footpath by Coach & Horses pub, Ickenham
01895 254159
April-December, 1st Sat in month 12-5.30pm

Roxbourne Park
Field End Road, Ruislip
Opposite Clay Pigeon pub. 2-5pm Sundays, Easter-Oct

Ruislip Lido Railway
Ruislip Lido. 01895 622595
Train from play area to Waters Edge pub.
Weekends all year, weekdays school holidays.
Also Santa specials

Further afield

Buckinghamshire Railway Centre
Quainton Road Station, Quainton
01296 655450
Steam, diesel, Santa and Thomas days. Also
Birthday parties

Chinnor & Princes Risborough Railway
Chinnor, Bucks. 01844 353535 talking timetable
Special events such as Thomas, Easter, Teddy
Bear and Hallowe'en. Santa specials

Didcot Railway Centre
Didcot, Oxon. 01235 817200
Collection of old engines, occasional 'steam' days

Leighton Buzzard Railway
Page's Park Station, Billington Road,
Leighton Buzzard. 01525 373888
Steam events and Xmas trains

Nene Valley Railway
Wansford Station, Stibbington, Peterborough
01780 784404

travel companies specialising in children

(see also ski companies, travel with kids)

The Bosman Safari Company
07880 732115

Club Med
020 7581 1161
Brochures: 01455 852 202

Eurocamp
0870 901 9451

EuroVillages
01606 787776

Mark Warner
0870 848 0482

Thomson Holida
0870 550 2555

travel with kids

There are Baby Directory guides to great
swathes of the UK. See our order form at the
beginning of the book, or check out our
website at **www.babydirectory.com**.
Here are some other publications and websites

Edinburgh for Under Fives

Kids Gids
Guide to Amsterdam

Le Paris des tout-petits
Guide to Paris

www.babygoes2.com
01273 230669

www.travellingwithchildren.co.uk
01684 594831

tuition

The Student Support Centre
0800 132277

Potters Bar
Sylvia Knight
01707 658636

Watford
Sylvan Learning Centre
77-79 High Street
01923 253525

vaccinations

www.immunisation.org.uk
020 7972 3807

www.uvig.org
UK industry vaccine industry group

JABS (Justice, Awareness & Basic Support)
020 8204 3865

wellington boots

St Albans Wellibank
01727 839770
Exchange your child's old wellies for a new size (or give a small donation)

welsh

Welsh Playgroup
020 8965 3585

web sites

www.babydirectory.com
Directory, bookshop, encyclopaedia, nanny agency, links to thousands of other baby/child related companies…

water births

If planning a hospital delivery, check with your local hospital for their facilities and policies on water birth *(see hospitals: NHS, hospitals, private)*

SPLASHDOWN WATER BIRTH SERVICES LTD
0870 44 44 403
splashdown@ukonline.co.uk
www.waterbirth.co.uk
Nationwide birth pool hire. Videos, books, cassettes, midwives study days

Birth Works
14-15 Fiddlebridge Industrial Centre, Hatfield
01707 880333

Gentle Water Birthing Pools
50 North Way, Lewes, E.Sussex. 01273 474927
www.gentlewater.co.uk

An exciting new concept!

Teach baby signing the fun way
Baby music groups
with a difference !

With action-songs and nursery rhymes,
Sing and Sign teaches
simple signing for hearing babies,
enabling communication before speech

If you can sing in tune
and have a lively personality you could
Run your own Sing and Sign classes

Flexible hours
Comprehensive training
Ongoing support
Lesson plans
Own area
Low start-up cost/high returns

**Learn more about us
visit www.singandsign.com**
Call for an information pack **01273-550587**

YOGA IN PREGNANCY &
CHILDBIRTH

POSTNATAL YOGA

MOTHER & BABY YOGA

CHILDREN'S YOGA

YOGA AND YOGA THERAPY

BABY MASSAGE

For group and individual sessions
contact
Jyoti Gudka BRCP
(Sivananda trained Yoga teacher -
YBT trained Yoga Therapist)
020 8952 5965

working opportunities

SING & SIGN
01273 550587
www.singandsign.com
Run your own music groups teaching
established baby signing programme

Usborne Books at Home
020 8954 9376

yoga in pregnancy or for children

(see also antenatal teachers)

British Wheel of Yoga
01529 306851
Contact for list of teachers

**JYOTI GUDKA, B.R.P.C. YOGA
Harrow area
020 8952 5965**
Yoga for Pregnancy, Childbirth and Postnatal.
Mother & baby, children's yoga

**YOGA FOR PARENTING
(JULIE THOMAS)
St Albans
07779 032166
www.yoga4parenting.com**
Pregnancy, baby-yoga/massage, post-natal,
Active-birth workshops, well-woman yoga

Bishops Stortford
Isla Ball
01279 813413

Yoga
Parsonage Hall
01279 834670

Bushey Heath
Shelia Kaufman
020 8950 8322

Cambridge
Sharon Honig
01763 262906

Enfield
Lola Alcaraz-Perez
020 8804 0328

Harrow
Waldron Studios
020 8423 7635

Hillingdon Hospital
Pauline Scanlon
01895 851310

Hitchin
Hitchin Natural Therapy Centre
3-4 High Street
01462 459020

Kings Langley
Christine Shaw
07939 091023

Rayners Lane
Monica Burton
020 8422 0402

Royston
Billie France
01763 262683

Sue Maloney
Royston Complementary Health Centre
01763 247440

Tring
Julie Cade
01442 826754

Ware
Ware Centre for Yoga, Arts & Healing
Sucklings Yard, Church Street
01920 466567

Watford
Karen Patrick
020 8882 5996

Please say you saw the ad in
The Local Baby Directory

ZOOS

(see also farms, outings, parks & open spaces, playgrounds)

Herts

Broxbourne
Paradise Wildlife Park
White Stubbs Lane. 01992 470490
Animals plus indoor and outdoor play areas, railway, and café

Royston
Shepreth Wildlife Park
Station Road, Shepreth. 09066 800031 (info line @ 25p min)
Also adventure playground, pony rides and cafe

Bedfordshire

Whipsnade Wild Animal Park
Whipsnade, Nr Dunstable. 0990 200123
Includes animal displays (sealions, birds) train ride, large adventure playground. Café and picnic facilities

Woburn Safari Park
Woburn. M1 Junction 13. 01525 290407
Drive-through wildlife park with rhinos, monkeys, elephants, giraffes and more. Pets corner and adventure playground

East Sussex

Drusilla's Park
Alfriston. 01323 870234
One mile N of Alfriston, on A27 between Eastbourne & Brighton. Highly recommended

Essex

Saffron Waldren
Mole Hall Wildlife Park
Widdington
01799 542408

zoos (cont.)

Hampshire

Marwell Zoological Park
Colden Common, Winchester. 01426 943163
B2177, 6 miles sough of Winchester from Jct 11,
M3

London

Battersea Park Zoo
Battersea Park, North Carriage Drive, SW11
Lots of monkeys, cow, smaller mammals,
kangaroos etc. Poor café.

London Zoo
Regents Park, NW1. 020 7722 3333

Oxfordshire

Cotswold Wildlife Park
Burford. 01993 823006
Exotic wildlife from lions to rhinos. Adventure
playground, children's farmyard, railway and
café. On A361

Surrey

Birdworld and Underwater World
Holt Pound, Farnham. 01420 22140

notes

notes